*LEGAL ASPECTS OF MARKETING*

*PERSPECTIVES IN MARKETING SERIES*

Robert D. Buzzell and Frank M. Bass, CONSULTING EDITORS

Howard   *LEGAL ASPECTS OF MARKETING*

# LEGAL ASPECTS OF MARKETING

*MARSHALL C. HOWARD*
*Professor of Economics*
*University of Massachusetts*

*McGRAW-HILL BOOK COMPANY*
*New York   San Francisco   Toronto   London*

II

*To Agnes*

# EDITORS' PREFACE

This book is the first of a series dealing with selected topics in marketing. The overall plan of the series includes two types of books: concise treatments of major subject or problem areas, such as marketing channels, pricing, and consumer behavior; and expositions of relatively new developments and techniques, such as experimental research methods. It is our hope that the series will provide an effective means of communicating important ideas in a more flexible format than that provided by traditional texts or collections of readings.

Professor Howard's analysis of the legal aspects of marketing is a concise but complete treatment of this important subject. No marketing manager can fulfill his responsibilities without attention to the legal regulations within which he must operate and to the possible legal consequences of his actions. By the same token, the student preparing for a career in marketing should develop an understanding of the law and of the social and political factors lying behind it.

The American economy has been aptly described as a "mixed system." While we still adhere to free enterprise as a basic principle, governmental agencies participate in the economic process in a variety of ways to shape business

decisions. On some occasions, the role of the government becomes excessive and burdensome—or, at least, so it seems to those
most directly concerned. On the whole, however, the mixed system has worked well and has probably been an effective compro-
mise between untrammeled private enterprise and the oppressive
forms of state control that have evolved in some other societies.
In any event, it seems likely that legal regulation of business,
and especially of marketing decisions, has become a permanent
fixture of the American scene. Professor Howard describes the
main provisions of the laws in this sphere, explains how they
have been interpreted and applied, and indicates how they
affect the task of the marketing executive and the marketing
process itself.

This book will be useful to practitioners and students of
marketing in several ways. Teachers of basic collegiate courses
in marketing will find that the book supplements and enriches
the coverage provided by most textbooks. Courses in business
law may also be stimulated by the exploration of the effects of
legal regulation in this area of business management. In advanced courses, the book can serve as an introduction to the
detailed study of legal regulation and its historical background.
At the end of each chapter, Professor Howard has supplied lists
of references for further reading.

For the marketing executive, the book provides a concise
reference source for checking the provisions of the most important laws and their applications to specific marketing policies.

This book represents the synthesis of several years' study by
Professor Howard, who has long been concerned with the legal
aspects of marketing. We think that the fruits of his labor
justify his efforts, and we are proud to have it appear as the
first in this series.

*Robert D. Buzzell*
*Frank M. Bass*

# PREFACE

In the American economy a legal framework places competition, including the various aspects of the marketing process, under regulatory control. The body of law which makes up this framework has expanded over the years with the passage of new legislation, and its applicability to trade has become more extensive through decisions made by enforcement agencies and the courts. The full extent to which this law is a force with which the marketer must reckon is frequently not recognized. This book is an effort to survey and synthesize for the convenience of the student, teacher, and businessman the relevant law, its interpretation and application, and the agencies which enforce it.

It is important for the marketing manager and students of the subject to understand fully how the law applies to marketing decisions which must be made. Few facets of marketing, whether of buying or selling, escape the surveillance and jurisdiction of the law. The attitude of the law toward price-making, for example, is of utmost signficance to the marketer. Can the businessman discuss prices with his competitors? Under what conditions can resale prices be controlled by a manufacturer or distributor? What price practices are considered deceptive? When can a seller meet the prices of his competitors on a discriminatory basis? How are quantity discount schedules, functional discounts, or brokerage, affected by the law? How does the law exercise control over the granting of promotional allowances or services to customers?

The marketing manager must also know the law concerning distribution. Exclusive dealing, requirements contracts, tying arrangements, and territorial distributorships may not be legal under certain circumstances. The use of joint ventures and the practice of business reciprocity are subject to possible legal control. A firm is not always legally free to purchase a customer's or rival's assets or capital stock. Nor can a firm acquire by purchase the right to produce and sell a new product, even for purposes of diversification or extension of product line, with complete legal impunity.

Almost all businessmen know that false advertising and misrepresentation are unfair methods of competition which can be attacked under the law. What is often not known is the supporting body of legal precedent which defines more specifically the illegality of these practices. The same is true of other unfair methods of competition. This book presents the fundamentals of the legal background of unfair competition in order to provide a basis for better understanding. And where requirements for labeling are specific in the law itself, or are spelled out in rules formulated by an enforcement agency, these requirements or their source and the products involved are pointed out.

The book is organized so that, with the exception of the first and last chapters, it will be possible to read these materials in conjunction with others pertaining to similar, but nonlegal, aspects of marketing. Most of the articles listed in the further readings at the end of each chapter are selected from journals or magazines which are readily available. Legal references and a brief explanation of these references are made in Appendixes A and B to permit the reader to examine further the relevant statutes or decisions.

I wish to thank Prof. Theodore N. Beckman of The Ohio State University and Paul E. Bragdon, Esq., of New York City and the New York Bar for their critical and helpful comments.

All deficiencies are, of course, the responsibility of the author. I am indebted to Mrs. Doris R. Holden for skillful secretarial assistance and to my father, Prof. Stanley E. Howard, for assistance with the proofs.

*Marshall C. Howard*

All definitions are of ... the responsibility of the author ...

# CONTENTS

# 1

## *THE LEGAL FRAMEWORK*

Marketing has been defined in different ways by different writers. It clearly involves the processes by which goods and services flow from the producers to the ultimate consumers. Market research, product policy, price policy, determination of the channels of distribution to be utilized, and advertising and promotion all can be included in marketing. What we shall be concerned with in the following pages are the ways in which any of these elements of marketing are subjected to legal controls in the free enterprise competitive economy of the United States. The impact of the law on marketing is felt largely through those controls established to govern competition.

The theory of a free enterprise economic system is that competition, free from restraints, provides an optimum allocation of resources. The producer-seller must satisfy the customers' wants. To do this he must know the customers' wants and be able to satisfy them as well as or better than business rivals can. Competition can be in terms of price, quality, nature of the product or service, or conditions of sale. The successful producer-seller is the one who has been most skillful in researching the buyers' wants, in procuring the resources to satisfy those wants, in making the goods available in desired form to the users, and in promoting sales. Other things being equal, this is accomplished by offering the best-quality goods at the lowest prices and on the most convenient terms of sale and delivery. Competition forces the business rivals to provide the best for the least. The efficient firms will be profitable and survive; the inefficient will not.

The free enterprise system requires a legal framework to ensure that this competitive process is healthy and effective, for free and open competition has not been found to be an entirely natural phenomenon. Deficiencies may be present in two principal respects. First, the producers and sellers of goods have often felt that they can increase their profits if they restrain trade and prevent the full operation of the competition. The record is clear on this point. Restraints of trade may ultimately reach monopolistic proportions, involving either a single business firm or, more likely, a group of firms acting in concert. Division of markets and price-fixing schemes, for example, represent two of the chief tools of the monopolists. Likewise, freedom of entry of potential competitors may be prevented by restraints of trade. Such exclusion is the antithesis of free enterprise. This is where the antimonopoly or antitrust laws must be applied to restrain those who wish to restrain trade. These laws have applied with special force to the selling aspects of the marketing process.

The second area of business conduct where law must guide and control is that of deceptive competitive acts or practices. The consumer cannot always keep himself well informed with respect to the alternative goods or services available or the exact nature of the alternatives, and some marketers may attempt to take advantage of this consumer ignorance to the detriment of both the consumer and the other competitors. Such conduct does not usually tend to create monopolistic situations; rather, it is unfair to competitors and requires that buyers beware. Here legal rules attempt to keep the competition fair and protect both sellers and consumers.

Government regulation thus serves two groups: the consumers and the business competitors. The consumer is served by the efforts of the law to prevent monopoly and, consequently, the higher prices and lower quality that may accompany monopoly. The consumer benefits too by the elimination of market practices which deceive him in his buying. Business firms are also served in two ways: Market conduct by powerful business rivals which might deprive firms of free access to the marketplace is subject to regulatory control, and business competitors are protected from rivals who choose to resort to practices which may deceive consumers. Without regulation against deceptive selling tactics, those competitors who wished to avoid their use might not survive the competition on the basis of their efficiency; to survive, they might be forced to adopt similar tactics. In short, government regulation serves to maintain a healthy competition free of exclusion and deception. Much of the legal control over competition has been sought by business itself. It is not a case of government on the one hand against business on the other hand, although any one government suit may present that impression.

It is one thing to construct the general legal rules of the game. It is something else again to interpret the true nature of business behavior and conduct in the marketplace under various circumstances and to apply these rules accordingly. Some difficult questions concerning the nature of the functioning of markets are indeed raised. For example, in attempting to apply the antitrust laws, when is destruction of a competitor wilful and predatory, and when is it merely a matter of survival of the economic fittest? Each seller tries to outsell his competitor; suppose he does such a good job of it that he is the only seller left in the marketplace? Should a seller have the right to select his own customers under all circumstances? The facts are that in the United States economy there are firms of all sizes and degrees of vertical integration. If a large integrated firm as a source of basic raw materials or semifinished goods to the small nonintegrated firm were to refuse to sell to the latter, as might well happen in periods of shortage, the latter might then not be able to enter or might even be forced to retire from an industry. To force the large firm to sell to the small firm is to interfere with the freedom of business dealings of the large firm, yet to permit the large seller to refuse to sell to the small buyer may eliminate the small firm from the marketplace. One might argue that competition has been interfered with in either case.

Similar problems of interpretation arise in applying the legal rules of the game to deceptive acts or practices. Do advertising efforts truly inform the consumer of the nature of the goods that he is considering purchasing, or do they deceive him? It is quite evident that practically all sellers of goods from time to time are guilty of overstating the characteristics or qualities of their products. This can be attributable to a genuine belief in the inherent superiority of one's own products, or it may be due to deliberate efforts to make the consumer believe that one's goods are better than those of the competitors when the seller knows that this is not so. In other words, selling efforts may range all the way from simply informing the public, to puffing up the value of a product, to deception and false advertising. The latter two methods of competition are unfair not only to the competitor who is more scrupulous in his dealings with the consumer, but also, obviously, to the consumers themselves. Some cases of deception may be relatively harmless, but others may be seriously detrimental to the public.

## FEDERAL LEGISLATION AGAINST RESTRAINTS OF TRADE AND MONOPOLY

The Sherman Antitrust Act of 1890, a landmark of Federal legislation, established statutory public policy toward restraint of trade and monopoly in interstate and foreign commerce. It was the first piece of Federal legislation that provided a general statement of public policy in the matter of preserving freedom of entry and the maintenance of competition. Its now-famous provisions defend competition by declaring restraints of trade and monopolies to be misdemeanors. Section 1 condemns "every contract, combination . . . or conspiracy, in restraint of trade." Section 2 condemns monopolizing or attempts to monopolize. Both sections apply to interstate and foreign commerce.[1] Enforcement of the Sherman Antitrust Act is delegated to the Antitrust Division of the Department of Justice.

Even though negative in character, the Sherman Antitrust Act was a positive step forward in regulating trade. The main intent of those fashioning the act was to codify the common law. But the common law itself was not a clear-cut body of doctrine. Generally speaking, agreements in restraint of trade such as price-fixing, pooling arrangements, cornering of the market, division of markets along territorial or commodity lines, or restric-

---

[1] For excerpts from the Sherman Antitrust Act and other basic antitrust laws, see Appendix B. For the legal citation for any of the Federal statutes referred to in this book, see Appendix A.

tion of sales had been treated simply as being unenforceable in the courts. Such practices as sales below cost, exclusive dealing, and tying arrangements had usually been deemed by the common-law courts to constitute legitimate market behavior even when employed to eliminate a competitor. And relief for third parties through damage suits had generally been obtainable only if the methods of the restraint were considered criminal or highly unorthodox. As for business combinations, the businessman had had little reason to fear a prosecution for conspiracy unless violence or fraud were involved. Finally, the common law had provided only a framework to permit private redress from private wrongs. Such a legal framework thus required private initiative and could hardly have been expected to constitute more than an implied statement of public policy.

In the latter part of the 1880s several states had passed antimonopoly laws, and some had adopted constitutional prohibitions in this matter. But the constitutional prohibitions were usually general, simply denouncing monopoly in principle. The state legislation attempted to reach those restrictive agreements which had been unenforceable at common law, but these state laws were not actively enforced. Limited funds and personnel available to the prosecuting authorities, the limited jurisdiction of the individual states, and a fear of driving industry from a state worked to deter active enforcement. Passage of the Sherman Act thus filled a large gap.

Two principal schools of thought have been advanced to explain the passage of the Sherman Act. One emphasizes the inadequacy of the common law and state antimonopoly laws, coupled with a growing opposition to "trusts" and a growing public demand for such legislation. The other has taken the position that the act was passed by Congress as a matter of political expediency and as a tactical move by interests seeking the passage of a tariff bill. But in any case the act was in accord with the American tradition of fair opportunity. Who could openly be in favor of monopoly when stated opinion was practically unanimous that "competition is the life of trade"? A similar public policy against combinations or conspiracies in restraint of trade, this time with respect to imports, was also declared in the antitrust amendment to the Wilson Tariff Act of 1894.

In 1914 two more acts of Congress were passed to strengthen competition. The principal purpose of this new legislation was to catch in their incipiency practices which might lead to monopoly. The first was the Federal Trade Commission Act which established the Commission of that name. Three years prior to this the United States Supreme Court had laid down the "rule of reason" with respect to interpretation of restraints of trade and monopolies under the Sherman Act.[2] Under this rule the Court's attitude was that restraints should be considered on their own merits, case by case, to determine whether they were reasonable (legal) or unreasonable (illegal). This was the Court's response to and interpretation of the phrase "every contract" in Section 1. There was a feeling that this wide leeway in interpretation placed in the hands of the courts considerably weakened the Sherman Act. The new Commission would now presumably be a body of specialists who might best be able to handle the economic and technical questions in antitrust matters. To support this thinking the Commission was given broad powers of investigation, jurisdiction over the enforcement of Section 5 of the act, which declared "unfair methods of competition" to be illegal, and the power to issue cease and desist orders. Over the years, and with amendment, Section 5 of the act has been interpreted broadly to reach not only those restraints of trade which might lead to monopoly but also those deceptive practices which injure a competitor or the consumer.

In a further attempt to supplement the Sherman Act, Congress also passed in 1914 the Clayton Act, "An Act to supplement existing laws against unlawful restraints and monopolies, and for other purposes." It, too, was an effort to meet the need "to arrest the creation of trusts, conspiracies, and monopolies in their incipiency and before consummation."[3] This act attempted to make the law more specific with respect to restraints. Three practices specifically mentioned were discrimination in price (Section 2), tying and exclusive agreements (Section 3), and acquisition of stock of another corporation (Section 7). These three practices

[2] *Standard Oil Co. of New Jersey et al. v. United States,* 221 U.S. 1 (1911).
[3] Senate Committee on the Judiciary, S. Rept. 698, 63d Cong., 2d Sess., 1914, p. 1.

were not worded so as to be illegal per se, but only "where the effect . . . may be to substantially lessen competition or tend to create a monopoly." This qualifying clause has compelled the enforcing authorities to develop their interpretations of its applicability. In a sense they have still had to resort to a rule of reason, but acceptance of a doctrine of "reasonable probability" in interpreting the word "may" does not require that the restraints of trade evidence actuality of injury to competition. It was certainly the intent of Congress to apply more stringent tests for measuring the legality of an economic arrangement than those to be applied under the Sherman Act. A fourth practice specifically mentioned was that of interlocking directorates (Section 8). Here definitions in the law were more clear-cut. No person shall be a director in any two or more corporations at the same time if any one of the corporations has capital, surplus, and undivided profits aggregating more than $1 million and if by virtue of their business and location of operations the corporations are competitors. Both the Federal Trade Commission and the Department of Justice were given jurisdiction over the Clayton Act.

Section 2, the price discrimination section of the Clayton Act, underwent major revision in 1936. The impact of the depression on business and the growing competition of chain stores and other big buyers with their large buying power were prime factors in encouraging this new legislation. Large buyers were demanding and receiving price preferences on their purchases. Threats to take their business elsewhere or to do their own manufacturing enabled some buyers to obtain concessions not made available to smaller buyers. In some instances, demands for brokerage led to preferential concessions. The Great Atlantic & Pacific Tea Co. collected brokerage through its wholly-owned subsidiary, the Atlantic Commission Co., which collected a commission or brokerage on all produce handled and then delivered 70 per cent of that produce to A & P's retail stores.[4] It was felt that the differences in prices paid by large and small buyers were so discriminatory as to imperil the existence of small business-

---

[4] Federal Trade Commission, *Final Report on the Chain-Store Investigation,* S. Doc. 4, 74th Cong., 1st Sess., 1935, p. 27.

men. The result was the passage of the Robinson-Patman Act,
sometimes known as the Price Discrimination Chain Store Act.

In essence, the Robinson-Patman Act was designed to restrain price discrimination in such a manner as to secure equality
of business opportunities, especially for buyers. Whereas Section
2 of the Clayton Act in practice had been chiefly concerned with
a showing of a general injury to competition, Congress saw importance in the injury to the victims of discrimination. With this
in mind Section 2 was reworded and broadened to include the
words "prevent competition with any person." Another section
of the Robinson-Patman Act (Section 3) also made it a criminal
offense to sell goods at unreasonably low prices in order to destroy competition or eliminate a competitor. Section 2 was also
enlarged to provide the Federal Trade Commission with the
right to establish limits on quantity discounts, to forbid brokerage allowances except to independent brokers, and to prohibit
promotional allowances or the furnishing of services or facilities
except where made available to all "on proportionally equal
terms." The designers of the law, aiming to strengthen the precautionary element in antitrust and to afford greater equality of
opportunities, thus gave consideration to the individual competitor as well as to competition in general.

A major loophole in Section 7 of the Clayton Act was finally
plugged by the 1950 Celler-Kefauver amendment, known as the
Antimerger Act, whereby acquisition of *assets* as well as acquisition of *stock* was declared illegal where the effect may be to substantially lessen competition or to tend to create a monopoly.
This amendment was needed for several reasons. First, a 1926
decision of the Supreme Court had declared that acquisition of
assets brought about by voting stock unlawfully acquired could
not be attacked under the Clayton Act.[5] Second, the original
Section 7 had not been viewed as being applicable to anything
except direct competition at the same (horizontal) level, thus
leaving the vertical relationship unassailed.[6] Third, the Sherman

---

[5] *Thatcher Manufacturing Co. v. Federal Trade Commission*, 272 U.S.
554 (1926).

[6] The Supreme Court proved this view to be unfounded in 1957 in
*United States v. E. I. du Pont de Nemours & Co. et al.*, 353 U.S. 586 (1957).

Act had proved to have limitations in its applicability to the merger, especially the vertical merger.[7] Fourth, a continuing number of mergers led to some fear of a growing economic concentration, especially concerning its effect on small business. The amended Section 7 removed the previous restrictions which had been inherent in the law by making it now applicable to ". . . any line of commerce in any section of the country" rather than only to the competition between the acquiring and the acquired corporations or to that "in any community." In short, the intent of Congress was to broaden the scope of the act in its capability of preventing an incipient lessening of competition.

Before turning to a new topic, it should be mentioned that some industries have their own little antitrust laws. The Packers and Stockyards Act of 1921, applying to handlers of meats and poultry, makes it unlawful to engage in or use any unfair, unjustly discriminatory, or deceptive practices or devices; and manipulation of prices or conspiracies to apportion territories are illegal. The Federal Alcohol Administration Act of 1935 outlaws exclusive dealing and interlocking directorates in businesses involving alcoholic beverages where these practices effect a substantial lessening of trade. The Revenue Act of 1916 contains antidumping provisions which do not permit selling *imported* goods at substantially less than their market value or wholesale price with the intent of destroying or injuring an industry in the United States, or of preventing the establishment of an industry in the United States, or of restraining or monopolizing trade. The Tariff Act of 1930 has a provision declaring unfair methods of competition and unfair acts in the importation of articles unlawful where the effect or tendency is to destroy or substantially injure an industry or to restrain or monopolize trade.

Finally, it should be mentioned that the criminal code is specifically applicable to our free enterprise economy in order to keep transactions truly free of restraints of trade. The Antiracketeering Act of 1948 condemns obstructions to commerce by robbery, extortion, or threats of physical violence to persons or property.

---

[7] See especially *United States v. Columbia Steel Co. et al.,* 334 U.S. 495 (1948).

## FEDERAL LEGISLATION AGAINST DECEPTIVE PRACTICES

As we have mentioned, the "unfair methods of competition" of Section 5 of the Federal Trade Commission Act of 1914 was interpreted as including deceptive practices. Where injury to a competitor could be shown through misrepresentation or false advertising, such practices could be attacked under this law. But specific protection in behalf of the public had to await the passage of the 1938 Wheeler-Lea Act. This amendment changed the wording of Section 5 to include "unfair or deceptive acts or practices." No longer did injury to a competitor first have to be shown before the public interest could be protected.

Actually, one of the earliest pieces of Federal legislation passed in an effort to protect the consumer was the Food and Drug Act of 1906 which forbade the misbranding of foods and drugs. Cosmetics and therapeutic devices were also added to the coverage by the Federal Food, Drug, and Cosmetic Act of 1938. These acts have given the Food and Drug Administration control over the misbranding (as well as the adulteration) of such products. Misbranding exists where the labeling (or packaging) is false or misleading or omits important required information about harmful conditions of use. The enforcing authorities can require full disclosure; half-truths are not enough. Jurisdiction over the false advertising of foods, drugs, devices, and cosmetics (as distinct from labeling) was given specifically to the Federal Trade Commission by the Wheeler-Lea Act of 1938. Such advertisements are false when they mislead in a material respect, such as by failing to reveal consequences of use.

Special legislation designed to control deceptive practices with respect to specific goods or services or industries has also been passed from time to time. Disclosure of identity, composition, quality, or the presence of harmful ingredients has been required for such products as insecticides and fungicides, seeds, animal and human viruses, serums, toxins, horse meat, caustic poisons, and alcoholic beverages. The import trade practices provisions of the Tariff Act of 1930 require that imported articles or the containers they come in must be marked so as to show clearly the country of origin. The Perishable Agricultural Commodities Act of 1930 is supposed to prevent unfair and fraudulent practices in the marketing of perishable agricultural goods; it condemns false or misleading statements and misrepresentation by stamps, labels, or marks, and it does not permit unfair, unreasonable, discriminatory, or deceptive practices in weighing and counting. The Federal Alcohol Administration Act of 1935 condemns commercial bribery, deceptive labeling, and misleading advertising with respect to alcoholic beverages. The Securities Act of 1933 provides the potential investor with protection against deceptions relating to new issues of corporate securities. The Federal Aviation Act of 1958 condemns unfair or deceptive practices, such as misleading advertising, by air carriers. The Federal Hazardous Substances Labeling Act of 1960 is designed to control the labeling of packages of hazardous substances intended or suitable for household use.

The garment industry has been singled out for special attention, since the consumer is generally ignorant of the nature of materials and fibers, especially synthetics. The Federal Trade Commission has been given jurisdiction over three acts which provide for compulsory labeling requirements for products of this industry, with authority to draw up the implementing rules and regulations. These acts are the Wool Products Labeling Act of 1939, the Fur Products Labeling Act of 1951, and the Textile Fiber Products Identification Act of 1958.

The Flammable Fabrics Act of 1953, also enforced by the Federal Trade Commission, is in a somewhat different category of law. This act prohibits outright the manufacture or sale of any article of wearing apparel or fabric which is so highly flammable that it is dangerous when worn by individuals. Such manufacture or sale is deemed to be an unfair method of competition and an unfair and deceptive act. Injunctive and condemnation procedures and fines and imprisonment are provided for in this act.

Special legislation which influences the marketing of automobiles has also been passed. The Automobile Information Disclosure Act of 1958 requires that automobile dealers affix to new cars the manufacturer's suggested retail price of the automobile so that the prospective buyer can make a more intelligent decision about which car to buy in terms of price.

It is clear, then, that Congress has found a need for and has passed several pieces of legislation to preserve honest competition and to protect the consumer. Such legislation has come into being usually only after flagrant abuses have become too commonplace to be acceptable or after members of the public have been seriously injured. Section 5 of the Federal Trade Commission Act, however, remains the principal buttress of this regulatory effort with respect to goods in general. Written in general terms, as is true of the Sherman Act, it can be applied where the Commission and the courts feel it necessary.

### EXEMPTIONS FROM ANTITRUST LAWS

The sales of certain kinds of products and certain conditions under which products are sold have been exempted from the Federal antitrust laws. We do not intend to analyze every one of these situations in detail, but simply to mention them to indicate their existence.

The Capper-Volstead Act of 1922 permits persons engaged in the production of agricultural products as farmers to act together in associations to process and market such goods. The Cooperative Marketing Act of 1926 enables these same persons collectively to acquire, interpret, and disseminate crop and market information. Marketing agreements between the Secretary of Agriculture and processors, producers, associations of producers, and others handling agricultural products are exempt from antitrust by the Agricultural Marketing Agreement Act of 1933. Voluntary export trade associations carry exemption from the Sherman Act through the Webb-Pomerene Export Trade Act of 1918 as long as they are encouraging the extension of foreign trade but not fixing prices in domestic trade or restraining the trade of a competitor. The Fishermen's Collective Marketing Act of 1934 permits associations of fishermen or planters of aquatic products to meet together to permit more equal bargaining in their selling to dealers and processors, although the Secretary of Interior can issue cease and desist orders if prices become "unduly enhanced." Associations of marine insurance companies are exempt from antitrust under the Merchant Marine Act of 1920. Voluntary agreements which contribute to national defense may be exempted by the President under the terms of the Defense Production Act of 1950.

An exemption from antitrust legislation which has had an extensive influence on the marketing of such goods as drugs, cosmetics, and appliances is that which permits "fair trade" contracts under which a manufacturer may set minimum resale prices for branded goods. Fair trade legislation originates with the states, but Federal legislation has been passed to make what is lawful in intrastate commerce also lawful in interstate commerce.

Patent monopolies are, of course, legal under the patent laws enacted under the power granted by the U.S. Constitution.[8] But a patent monopoly cannot be extended to cover nonpatented goods nor can it be used as the basis of monopolistic agreements with competitors. Similarly, under the terms of the Lanham Trademark Act of 1946 trademarks can be the rightful owner's exclusive (monopolistic) property unless obtained fraudulently or used to deceive or to violate the antitrust laws. The Federal Trade Commission is authorized to institute proceedings before the Commissioner of Patents for cancellation of the registration of marks where grounds exist for such action.

### STATE AND LOCAL LEGISLATION

About one-half of the states have constitutional provisions against trusts or monopolies. They usually take the form of simply condemning such combinations and perhaps declaring that the legislature should pass the necessary legislation. With very few exceptions the states have some form of statutory provision against combinations, conspiracies, or restraints of trade. Some of these statutes are general; others provide rules against such practices as price-fixing, sales below cost, price discrimination, tying contracts, and exclusive dealing.

Price discrimination is frequently singled out by states for special statutory treatment; where it is not, it almost invariably receives attention either in the statutes against monopolies and restraints of trade or in unfair sales practices acts. The price discriminations declared illegal are either those which are simply "unfair" or those which have the purpose or effect of destroying a competitor or substantially lessening or preventing competition or tending to create a monopoly. Some industries or products are

[8] Art. I, sec. 8, clause 8.

also frequently designated for special treatment with respect to discrimination in price. Most frequently found in this category are insurance,[9] dairy and farm products, alcoholic beverages, and petroleum products.

With only a few exceptions, state antitrust laws have not been actively enforced; state legislation, rather, has often been directed toward, or had the effect of, limiting competition.[10] The states have been active in passing resale price maintenance legislation which permits the manufacturers of branded goods to set minimum resale prices of those goods. These fair trade acts have from time to time been declared unconstitutional, but in 1963 80 per cent of the states had such statutes which were still constitutional. State unfair sales practices acts, as general business sales-below-cost laws aimed at maintaining retail prices at levels sufficient to yield retailers and/or wholesalers a certain margin of profit, are on the statute books of somewhat over one-half of the states, but they have not been actively enforced. Some products, such as milk, alcoholic beverages, cigarettes, and gasoline, are singled out for special price control legislation by some states. Chain-store taxes, whose rates are sometimes progressive with the number of stores in the chain but which are relatively insignificant today, in the past at least have been aimed at protecting the small independent businessman from the competition of the large chain stores. Some states and municipalities have blue laws, which prohibit selling on Sunday. At least one state has prohibited the use of trading stamps, and others have restricted their use to some degree.

In certain occupations, such as accounting, architecture, law, barbering, and various occupations relating to medicine, just to mention a few, entry is sometimes limited by regulation. Whereas good public reason may be cited in favor of limiting entry in these occupations, regulation may nevertheless result in

[9] The McCarran-Ferguson Act of 1945 states that the regulation of the business of insurance by the states is in the public interest and that the Sherman Antitrust Act, the Clayton Act, and the Federal Trade Commission Act would be applicable to the insurance business only to the extent that such business is not regulated by state law.

[10] See Mark S. Massel, *Competition and Monopoly: Legal and Economic Issues,* The Brookings Institution, Washington, D.C., 1962, pp. 64–70.

limiting the number of competitors, and thus competition, in a given market.

Restrictions on the interstate marketing of goods have resulted from limitations on imports of certain types of out-of-state goods and from various special grading, labeling, and packaging requirements which are not uniform among the states. Laws which were passed as public health and sanitation measures or to ensure that the public is properly informed or protected may have been designed to restrain or at least result in restraining interstate trade. But the full extent and effect of such trade barriers has not been evaluated.

Most of the states have laws designed to ensure truth in advertising. Some states have laws against bait advertising and misleading pricing and local ordinances exist to ban deceptive advertising and selling; but many of these laws are ineffective and enforcement is often negligible.

## ENFORCEMENT PROCEDURES OF THE DEPARTMENT OF JUSTICE

The two principal agencies responsible for enforcing Federal antitrust legislation are the Antitrust Division of the Department of Justice and the Federal Trade Commission. The Antitrust Division is concerned with antitrust cases filed under the Sherman and Clayton acts. It uses court litigation to prosecute violations of the law, and in the decade between 1952 and 1961 it filed an average of fifty-three cases a year.[11] Price-fixing cases account for about two-thirds of the case load. Civil proceedings generally outnumber the criminal.

In response to complaints by businessmen and after investigation by the Federal Bureau of Investigation, the Antitrust Division initiates action in the district courts. In criminal proceedings under the Sherman Act, if the government wins its case, it can be appealed by the defendant; if the government loses its case, no appeal is available. Conviction may bring penalties of fines or imprisonment. Fines may be as high as $50,000 for each convicted defendant, and individual corporation executives may be defendants as well as the corporation itself. Actual imprison-

---

[11] Department of Justice release, Jan. 22, 1962, p. 6.

ment of corporate executives is a phenomenon of the 1960s. The drawback to these criminal penalties is that they do not alter the basic industrial structure which may have been conducive to the offense in the first place. A conviction, however, does put a corporation in jeopardy of private damage suits. A business may sue under the antitrust laws, claiming injury from the restraint of trade, and if successful, win treble damages. A conviction in a government suit is prima facie, although not conclusive, evidence of guilt in such damage suits. Defendants thus might well prefer a settlement with the Justice Department either by signing a consent decree, under which they agree not to do certain things and the court puts its official stamp on these terms, or by entering a plea of *nolo contendere* and throwing themselves on the mercy of the court. Neither of these last two procedures is, in the eyes of the law, an admission of guilt. The court, however, need not accept a plea of *nolo contendere* if it does not wish to do so.

The advantage to the Justice Department in entering a civil suit against a business is that it can request the court to issue a decree making some change which it feels is necessary to alter the basic industrial structure which had been contributing to the trade restraint. District courts have the power to issue an order requiring a corporation to divest itself of certain assets. Thus the du Pont chemical company has been ordered to divest itself of 63 million shares of General Motors capital stock.[12] Or the court can decree divorcement, as it did when it divorced the production-distribution facilities of the "Big Five" in the motion-picture industry from their exhibition facilities.[13] Or, even more drastically, it can dissolve a corporation, as it did in 1911, when the Supreme Court approved a lower court decree which broke up Standard Oil Co. of New Jersey by ordering it to distribute to its own stockholders the stocks which it held in thirty-three subsidiaries and by forbidding common officers and directors for the thirty-four companies.[14] An alternative procedure with respect

[12] *United States v. E. I. du Pont de Nemours & Co. et al.,* 366 U.S. 316 (1961), Trade Reg. Rep. par. 70,245 (1962).

[13] *United States v. Paramount Pictures et al.,* 334 U.S. 131 (1948).

[14] *Standard Oil Co. of New Jersey et al. v. United States,* 221 U.S. 1 (1911).

to altering the industrial structure is that represented by the United Shoe Machinery case of 1953, in which the court required the corporation to sell as well as lease its machines, to shorten and modify the terms of the leases, and to grant patent licenses to its competitors.[15] Divestiture, divorcement, and dissolution are the three D's of antitrust. By 1958 such remedies had been applied in less than a hundred cases, and the number of productive enterprises broken up was less than thirty.[16] Under less drastic action, a court may simply issue an injunction forbidding the defendant to engage in the same practice in the future.

## ENFORCEMENT PROCEDURES OF THE FEDERAL TRADE COMMISSION

The Federal Trade Commission is a bipartisan body of five commissioners of which not more than three are from the same political party. The term of office is seven years. The functions of the Commission are those of investigator and prosecutor-judge. As an investigating agency, it conducts investigations of business organization and conduct on its own initiative, upon the request of the President, Congress, government agencies, and the Attorney General, or upon referrals by the courts. Commission investigations have resulted in some significant studies of industrial structure, mergers, interlocking directorates, and international cartels. It also investigates as a result of complaints from the public alleging violations of the laws under its jurisdiction—the Federal Trade Commission Act, the Clayton Act, the Webb-Pomerene Export Trade Act, the Flammable Fabrics Act, and the wool, fur, and textile fiber products labeling acts. As a prosecutor-judge it utilizes administrative regulation, establishing rules and issuing cease and desist orders.

For the four-year period 1958 through 1961, the Federal Trade Commission issued approximately three complaints and cease and desist orders in deceptive practices cases to every one issued in antimonopoly cases. For the fiscal year 1961, 290 complaints and 265 cease and desist orders were issued in deceptive

[15] *United States v. United Shoe Machinery Corp.*, 110 F. Supp. 295 (1953).

[16] Clair Wilcox, *Public Policies toward Business,* Richard D. Irwin, Inc., Homewood, Ill., 1960, p. 113.

practices cases compared with 120 complaints and 103 orders to cease and desist in antimonopoly cases.[17] The great majority of the Commission's antimonopoly work is with Robinson-Patman Act discrimination cases. Mergers under the amended Section 7 of the Clayton Act also represent a substantial part of this case load, with thirty merger cases pending on June 30, 1961.

A formal complaint is the first step in the adjudicative proceedings of the Commission.[18] After the complaint has been issued, the motions, pleadings, conferences, and hearings are under the guidance of a hearing examiner. A decision of the hearing examiner, including a possible dismissal order, will then become final and be considered the decision of the Commission unless there is either a petition for review which is accepted by the Commission or the Commission itself issues an order placing the case on its own docket for review. In either of the latter two cases the Commission, after its own review, will issue the final order. This order becomes final unless the party against whom the order has been issued petitions for review in the court of appeals within sixty days. Compliance reports must also be filed within sixty days, or in cases involving the false advertising of food, drugs, devices, or cosmetics, within ten days. A violation of a final Commission order is subject to a civil penalty of not more than $5,000. For a continuing failure or neglect to obey an order, each day constitutes a separate offense.

Procedures may be shortened and expedited by use of the consent order. Where time, the nature of the proceeding, and the public interest permit, the Commission may notify the party of its intention to issue a complaint, along with the proposed form of order, prior to the actual issue of a complaint, with the result that an agreement may be reached in the form of a consent order. But once a complaint is filed, this consent-order procedure is not available. The consent order has the same legal standing as a decision reached under full adjudicative proceedings. A second possible procedure, that of the stipulation, has not been used since the middle of 1961. Under this procedure no formal com-

[17] Federal Trade Commission, *Annual Report,* 1961, p. 34.
[18] See latest edition of Federal Trade Commission, *Rules of Practice, Procedures and Organization* for details on procedure.

plaint was issued, but the party challenged by the Commission agreed not to engage in a certain practice. The stipulation, unlike the consent order, had no legal force.

Such procedures are negative; they simply order a party to cease doing what he has been doing. The Commission, however, on the assumption that businessmen will be less likely to violate the law if they are provided with more detailed rules as to what is expected of them, has established some positive procedures. Thus it conducts trade practice conferences at which members of the Commission and a particular industry meet and discuss rules of guidance proposed for the members of that industry. The *trade practice rules* drawn up as a result of these conferences are advisory and are only for the guidance of the industry members in their efforts to comply with the laws administered by the Commission; in official complaints the Commission must charge violation of the statutory provisions upon which the rules are based, not violation of the rules themselves. These rules are sometimes classified into two groups. Group I rules define practices which the Commission feels violate the law. In this category are often found various forms of deception or misrepresentation and such illegal practices as price-fixing, and sales below cost and discriminations with intent to suppress competition. Some of these rules have become standardized and appear in identical form in several different industry trade practice rules. The "free goods" rule, which establishes the permissible context in which the word "free" can be used in advertising, and the "push-money" rule, concerning money payments to customers' employees, are cases in point. Group II rules simply reflect the views of the industry on what practices are desirable or undesirable. For example, a rule may condemn unwarranted return of merchandise or may recommend the maintenance of accurate records. Although a rule may be favored by an industry, the Commission will not accept it if it believes that the proposed rule sanctions any practice which the Commission believes is contrary to law; for what businessmen may consider to be conducive to sound business methods may actually be conducive to restraints upon full and open competition.

Under new procedures established in 1962 the Commission may draw up *trade regulation rules,* which express its experience and judgment about the substantive requirements of the statutes it administers. Promulgated only after the public has had an opportunity to participate in the proceedings for their establishment, these rules may be relied upon by the Commission in adjudicative proceedings. The first trade regulation rule adopted by the Commission prohibits deceptive size designations for sleeping bags.

A second positive approach used by the Commission is the preparation of guides which are in essence the Commission's interpretation of the laws administered by it with respect to certain business practices. Actual prosecutions, however, still must come under the provisions of the law itself. Some of these guides apply to specific industries, such as the Cigarette and Tire Advertising Guides, and some apply to general business practices, such as the Guides on Deceptive Pricing and Advertising Allowances.

Finally, in this attempt to take a more positive approach, the Commission stands ready to give advisory opinions in advance about the legality of a proposed course of action by a business. These opinions are given with the right of the Commission to rescind or revoke its advice where, after further consideration, it feels it necessary. This practice of rendering advisory opinions was first initiated in 1962 and has had an overwhelming response from businessmen.[19]

Other procedures apply specifically to other laws assigned to the Commission to administer. Under the Wool Products Labeling Act, the Fur Products Labeling Act, the Flammable Fabrics Act, and the Textile Fiber Products Identification Act, the Commission has the duty of promulgating various rules and regulations which aid industry members in their compliance with the law, such as specifying various forms of misrepresentation. The substantive rules promulgated under these laws have the force and effect of law. The Commission also has the power to apply to a district court for injunctive relief in cases arising under these acts; and with respect to the first three acts mentioned, it can seek condemnation in the courts. Injunctions can also be sought in cases involving misrepresentation of food, drugs, devices, or cosmetics.

[19] Federal Trade Commission, *Annual Report*, 1962, p. 37.

## LEGAL FRAMEWORK: THEORY AND PRACTICE

It should be clear to the reader after this summary introduction to the legal framework surrounding the free enterprise system of the United States that freedom to transact business is subject to certain limitations. Marketers are limited in their buying and selling efforts not only by the impersonal market mechanism of demand and supply but also by the laws with which they must comply as interpreted and administered by the enforcement agencies and the judicial system.

The theory of the antitrust and antideceptive practices laws is to strengthen competition by removing obstructions to competition and by providing greater fairness to the competitor and to the consumer. The law, negative in character, is supposed to assure that enterprise is truly free to all and not just to a few. This is theory. The disagreements among lawyers, economists, and representatives of the government as to how and to what degree these legal prohibitions should be applied indicate that the lines for government action are not always perfectly clear-cut.

Disagreement among the analysts arises for three possible reasons. First, the laws, typically, are general. This can hardly be avoided. They can state only the general principle. The changing methods of business operate, as a rule, to discourage the making of laws that are too specific. Second, the laws themselves, being general in their wording, are subject to interpretation, and they must be applied to industries which are imperfectly competitive. Firms in competition are not all the same size in terms of assets, sales, or financial strength. This is inevitable. The analyst who uses the economic model of pure or perfect competition will remain constantly frustrated in his effort to fashion the public policy of control. A "workable" sort of competition, in which all is not perfectly black or white, must be adopted as his measuring stick. Third, some of the laws are written in a form which allows for an interpretation which provides apparent favor to some sectors of the economic structure. Is small business, for example, to be assured a place in the economic system? Are the exemptions from antitrust economically justified? The very meaning and nature of free competition is

subject to dispute as soon as we begin to debate the meaning
and limits of the word "free."

## SUGGESTIONS FOR FURTHER READING

The background for the passage of basic antitrust laws is available in Donald
Dewey, *Monopoly in Economics and Law*, Rand McNally & Company, Chicago, 1959, chaps. IX and X (common law); Hans B. Thorelli, *The Federal
Antitrust Policy*, The Johns Hopkins Press, Baltimore, 1955, part I (Sherman Act); Gerard C. Henderson, *The Federal Trade Commission*, Yale University Press, New Haven, Conn., 1924, chap. 1; David D. Martin, *Mergers
and the Clayton Act*, University of California Press, Berkeley, Calif., 1959;
and Corwin D. Edwards, *The Price Discrimination Law*, The Brookings Institution, Washington, D.C., 1959, chaps. 1 and 2 (Robinson-Patman Act). Early
state antitrust legislation is discussed in Henry R. Seager and Charles A.
Gulick, Jr., *Trust and Corporation Problems*, Harper & Brothers, New York,
1929, chap. XVII.

Various problems of antitrust administration, litigation, and negotiation
are discussed in *Report of the Attorney General's National Committee to
Study the Antitrust Laws*, 1955, chap. VIII; and Mark S. Massel, *Competi-
tion and Monopoly: Legal and Economic Issues*, The Brookings Institution,
Washington, D.C., 1962, chap. 5. Articles on particular issues are Milton S.
Goldberg, "The Consent Decree," *Business Topics*, Michigan State University,
Summer, 1960; Seth M. Dabney, "Antitrust Consent Decrees: How Protective
an Umbrella?" *Yale Law Journal*, June, 1959; Note in the *Yale Law Journal*,
"The Admissibility and Scope of Guilty Pleas in Antitrust Treble Damage
Actions," March, 1962; and Walter Jensen, Jr. and Harold A. Wolf, "A Legal
and Economic Note on Price-Fixing," *Business Topics*, Spring, 1962 (treble-
damage suits). The problem of the overlapping jurisdiction of the Federal
Trade Commission and the Department of Justice is discussed in Joseph W.
Burns, *A Study of the Antitrust Laws*, Central Book Co., New York, 1958,
chap. III.

# 2

# PRICE-MAKING

Price-making is one of the most important functions performed in the business firm. Theoretically, the impersonal
market forces of demand and supply are said to determine
prices in the marketplace. This is true in a general sense.
But there are significant elements of imperfection in most
markets today, providing most sellers with some small
amount of control over price, at least in the short run. The
particular location of the seller, his relative size in the
marketplace, an element of uniqueness in the product, the
use of brand names and trademarks, the holding of a patent
right, exceptional salesmanship—these are all factors which
may give a firm some ability to decide what the prices of its
products will be.

A firm's price policy can be a matter of concern to the
law. When independent business rivals get together to
determine prices, they are preventing the forces of competition within the industry from setting prices which will tend
to yield to the firms only a normal or reasonable profit.
Such joint action is monopolistic behavior and is illegal.
Exactly why collusive pricing is illegal, why some businesses
on occasion engage in the practice, what the symptoms and
costs are are matters discussed in this chapter. Although
collusive pricing by buyers is equally illegal, we shall use
the context of sellers, where the issue has been more in the
forefront, in our discussion.

There are two exceptions at law to the established principle that sellers must determine independently the prices they charge for the goods which they sell. First, the producer or distributor of branded goods may, under state fair trade laws, prescribe the prices below which the reseller may not sell such goods. Second, state sales below cost or minimum markup laws establish floors for prices below which resellers of goods cannot sell. These two exceptions are discussed at the end of this chapter. Federal statutes also regulate sales below cost, but these are more directly concerned with price discrimination, which is discussed in the following chapter.

### PRICE-FIXING IS ILLEGAL PER SE

Marketers must determine independently the prices of the goods or services they sell. For competitors to agree among themselves about the prices to be charged is illegal per se under the antitrust laws. Horizontal agreements on price, whether direct or indirect, and regardless of the means used, are in clear violation of the law. Those business firms which agree on prices have no excuse. They cannot argue, in defense, that prices are too low to yield a reasonable profit, or that market prices are too chaotic, or even that the price they are fixing is a reasonable price. They are, in the eyes of the law, conspirators. As stated by Chief Justice Warren of the Supreme Court in a 1956 decision:

> It has been held too often to require elaboration now that price fixing is contrary to the policy of competition underlying the Sherman Act and that its illegality does not depend on a showing of its unreasonableness, since it is conclusively presumed to be unreasonable. It makes no difference whether the motives of the participants are good or evil; whether the price fixing is accomplishd by express contract or by some more subtle means; whether the participants possess market control; whether the amount of interstate commerce affected is large or small; or whether the effect of the agreement is to raise or decrease prices.[1]

The Sherman Act is subject to the jurisdiction of the Department of Justice. This does not mean that the Federal Trade Commission is helpless to attack price-fixing. It has become a well-established legal principle that price-fixing is a per se unfair

---

[1] *United States v. McKesson & Robbins, Inc.,* 351 U.S. 305, 309–310 (1956).

method of competition which can be struck down under Section 5 of the Federal Trade Commission Act. State antitrust laws generally assume this same position against collusive price behavior. Indeed, thirty-three states expressly prohibit by statute price-fixing by business in general, and two other states have statutory provisions aimed at specific price-fixing combinations, one concerning the price of necessities, the other concerning the price of food and other necessaries. In addition, one state has a constitutional provision against price-fixing. Thus, price-fixers are clearly liable to attack by the guardians of antitrust. Price-fixing is a "hard core" offense; there is no uncertainty as to its illegality.

The Sherman Act does not specifically declare price-fixing to be illegal. Neither does the Federal Trade Commission Act. On first blush it would therefore seem that those found guilty of determining prices in concert might claim that the Federal law, written in general terms, is uncertain and that they did not know that they were violating the law. But the legal precedents are firmly established and date back to the turn of the century.

The per se illegality of price-fixing can be traced back to as early as 1897 in a decision of the Supreme Court in which the Sherman Act was strictly construed about the application and interpretation of the word "every" in Section 1.[2] Several railroads had reached agreement on the rates they were to charge. There was no room, said the court, to try to determine whether these rates were reasonable or not, for the statute declared "every" contract in restraint of trade to be illegal. A defense that the railroads were only attempting to avoid ruinous competition was therefore not acceptable. A similar position was taken and a similar defense overruled in another decision by the Supreme Court a year later in a second case involving joint rate-making by railroads.[3]

A third price-fixing case, in 1899, this time involving six leading manufacturers of iron pipe, was again decided in favor of the government.[4] The defense was the same as that in the two preceding cases: the sellers were only trying to avoid ruinous

---

[2] *United States v. Trans-Missouri Freight Assn.*, 166 U.S. 290 (1897).
[3] *United States v. Joint Traffic Assn.*, 171 U.S. 505 (1898).
[4] *United States v. Addyston Pipe & Steel Co.*, 175 U.S. 211 (1899).

competition among themselves in which price would be driven too low to be reasonable to themselves and the public. The reasoning of the court was different in this case, however. It was not the word "every" in Section 1 of the Sherman Act which was restrictive; it was just that the common law had restricted the application of the rule of reason to ancillary restraints and that all nonancillary restraints were condemned. If a seller were to sell his business to another manufacturer, an agreement of the seller of the business not to compete might be legally justified; otherwise the buyer might never have undertaken the purchase of the business. In such an instance, the agreement not to compete is only ancillary, or subordinate, to the agreement to sell the business. On the other hand, for existing producers to agree not to compete with each other in the sale of their products is a nonancillary or general restraint which is not permissible under the common law. So went the thinking of the court, and so was established precedent with respect to price-fixing agreements, which survived even the Supreme Court's acceptance in 1911 of the doctrine that a rule of reason should be applied to Sherman Act cases.[5] Price-fixing now was simply to be considered an unreasonable restraint of trade.

That price-fixing was not to be tolerated was made abundantly clear by the Supreme Court in the celebrated Trenton Potteries case in 1927. Here manufacturers and distributors representing 82 per cent of the vitreous pottery bathroom fixtures produced in the United States had agreed upon prices. Their defense was that, although they might have fixed prices, those prices were reasonable. The court refused to accept this idea.

> The aim and result of every price-fixing agreement, if effective, is the elimination of one form of competition. The power to fix prices, whether reasonably exercised or not, involves power to control the market and to fix arbitrary and unreasonable prices. The reasonable price fixed today may through economic and business changes become the unreasonable price of tomorrow.[6]

Although the manufacturers and producers represented 82 per cent of the market in the Trenton Potteries case, that large

---

[5] *Standard Oil Co. of New Jersey v. United States,* 221 U.S. 1 (1911).
[6] *United States v. Trenton Potteries Co. et al.,* 273 U.S. 392, 396 (1927).

market percentage was not a controlling factor in the decision. A 1933 decision involving a price agreement among 137 producers of bituminous coal did, however, throw some uncertainty into the matter of whether or not the market position of the sellers affected the legality of the agreement.[7] Producers representing 54.2 per cent of the bituminous coal mined in the Appalachian area planned to sell through an exclusive sales agency. The court held that although competition would be eliminated among these producers, there was still effective competition in the ultimate markets and that the group would have no control over market price. The court emphasized the presence of several special factors, such as excess capacity, the existence of "distress coal," and several destructive practices which, in total, added up to an industry in distress. But if there was any doubt about the legal status of price-fixing under the Sherman Act because of the Appalachian Coals or any other decision, it was thoroughly dispelled in 1940 in the Socony-Vacuum decision. In this decision all methods of price-fixing, whether direct or indirect, were condemned. Specifically, several major oil companies had set out to control price by controlling the supply on the market. To accomplish this certain independent (small) refiners were assigned as "dancing partners" to each member of this group of large refiners. The surplus or "distress" gasoline of these small refiners was then bought up by the large oil companies as needed in order to keep the price from falling. Said Justice Douglas:

> For over forty years this Court has consistently and without deviation adhered to the principle that price-fixing agreements are unlawful *per se* under the Sherman Act and that no showing of so-called competitive abuses or evils which those agreements were designed to eliminate or alleviate may be interposed as a defense. . . .
>
> The machinery employed by a combination for price-fixing is immaterial.
>
> Under the Sherman Act a combination formed for the purpose and with the effect of raising, depressing, fixing, pegging, or stabilizing the price of a commodity in interstate or foreign commerce is illegal *per se*.[8]

Any exchange of information among competitors is suspect, for the information may affect prices. The members of trade associations must be exceedingly careful at their meetings not to

[7] *Appalachian Coals, Inc. v. United States,* 288 U.S. 344 (1933).

[8] *United States v. Socony-Vacuum Oil Co.,* 310 U.S. 150, 218, 223 (1940).

discuss material which affects current or future prices. Even vertical price agreements, such as between producers and distributors, are illegal unless they are exempted by state and Federal resale price maintenance legislation (to be discussed later in this chapter).

## ECONOMIC CONDITIONS INDUCING PRICE-FIXING

Although price-fixing is illegal per se, price-fixing cases account for about two-thirds of the case load of the Antitrust Division of the Department of Justice, and the Federal Trade Commission also sometimes handles such cases. It would seem that human nature has not changed in the last two hundred years and that the father of economics, Adam Smith, was an acute observer of the business scene when he commented in 1776: "People of the same trade seldom meet together, even for merriment and diversion, but the conversation ends in a conspiracy against the public or in some contrivance to raise prices."[9]

An early twentieth-century version of gatherings at which industry members discussed prices was the "Gary dinners" held by Judge Gary of the U. S. Steel Corporation for members of the steel industry at irregular intervals until 1911. These dinners ceased when the government became suspicious of their purpose. But clandestine meetings to discuss prices have continued from time to time in many different industries, as evidenced by the successful government prosecutions right up to the present. The indictments in 1960 and eventual pleadings of guilty by the principal firms and certain corporate officers in the electrical-equipment industry have accented the prevalence of the phenomenon. Indeed, with respect to that industry it has been said that such conspiracies were "virtually an industry tradition."[10] Trade associations frequently have provided an implementing device to facilitate such meetings. Though hotel rooms are most frequently cited as locations, the finger has also been put on bars and golf courses. The proclivity toward price-fixing perhaps can best be summed up in the words of a corporation and trade association official in testimony before the Federal Trade Com-

[9] *Wealth of Nations,* Book I, chap. x, part II.
[10] John Q. Lawyer (pseudonym), "How to Conspire to Fix Prices," *Harvard Business Review,* March–April, 1963, p. 95.

mission in a price-fixing complaint involving the producers and distributors of chains and their trade association:

> I could go on and on and on—but I want to say that when any two businessmen get together, whether it is a Chain Institute meeting or a Bible class meeting, if they happen to belong to the same industry, just as soon as the prayers have been said, they start talking about the conditions in the industry, and it is bound definitely to gravitate, that talk, to the price structure in the industry. What else is there to talk about?[11]

Why has there been so much price-fixing, in spite of the fact that there is no legal defense for such business behavior? Where certain conditions of demand and supply are present, business firms realize that unless they act to try to control price, their profits are likely to suffer. A first requisite condition is that there be few enough producers in the industry to make a meeting and agreement mutually desirable and feasible. In the terminology of the economist, the structure of the industry must be that known as *oligopoly*. This means that there must be relatively few sellers, so few that they are quite aware of each other's existence and fully conscious of the impact their own pricing actions will have on the price behavior of the rivals and ultimately on the profits being earned in the industry.

Where the aggregate demand for the product is (felt to be) inelastic, a reduced market price for all sellers will lead only to lower profits for all. Sellers of basic steel, for example, generally feel that price reductions of their product would not lead to any significant increase in the quantity demanded because the demand for basic steel is one which is derived from the demand for such things as automobiles and commercial and industrial building construction. Yet if only one seller lowers his price, business will tend to flow toward that one seller, leaving the rival sellers with considerably reduced sales. All sellers, in other words, are motivated to maintain price at an existing, stable, profitable level. Whereas each of the sellers is aware of the danger of cut prices to his profits and may well act accordingly without any overt understanding being necessary, an agreement will provide insurance that each seller will price wisely in the interests of all. This is especially true where the oligopolists are not of equal size in

[11] *Chain Institute, Inc. et al.,* 49 F.T.C. 1041, 1082 (1953).

terms of the percentage of the market to which they sell and where the relatively small sellers are anxious to obtain a larger share of the market. Also, the more standardized the product, the greater the danger is that price-cutting will take on serious proportions; the more differentiated the product, the less each seller will tend to fear loss of sales if rivals lower their prices.

From the cost point of view, the larger the overhead costs of the firms in an industry, the more each seller will fear price-cutting. For the floor to prices in a retaliatory price war tends to be at the level of unit variable costs of production. When prices are driven below that level, it is more profitable to withdraw from production and selling, unless shut-down costs are prohibitive or it is vital to maintain customer relationships. To put it in another way, when price will not cover the labor and raw materials that go into a product, it will generally be more economical to shut down operations. On the other hand, selling is likely to continue even if price does not cover the total cost of a product as long as at least some contribution is being made toward the overhead costs. For some contribution is better than none. The more long-lived the plant and equipment (representing the overhead costs), the longer the cut prices (which do not cover all overhead costs) may persist. If the plant and equipment are not specialized and can be fairly easily converted to other uses, then of course, the dangers of price-cutting are minimized, for the producers can direct these resources into other more profitable uses if necessary.

Finally, price-cutting is unlikely to develop where there is no excess capacity of plant. Where demand is strong enough at existing prices to cause all plant to be fully utilized, there will be no inducement to cut prices. On the contrary, the producer-sellers may be asking themselves whether the demand is strong enough to enable them to raise price without losing any significant amount of business. In most of the heavy industries in the United States, however, there are recurring periods of excess capacity. For the economy and its industries are, have been, and probably always will be subject to the uncertainties of fluctuations of demand. In addition, expanding industries frequently build capacity today in order to meet tomorrow's demand. The result may well be chronic excess capacity.

The urge to engage in collusive price-making thus stems from the desire to avoid the price-cutting which undermines profits in periods of excess capacity. The individual members of the industry may well understand the dangers to profits inherent in price reductions, but any single firm may also think in terms of hoped-for gains if that firm were to be the only one to cut price, hoping that the other sellers would not meet the price reduction. This threat of individual action taken in the interests of the individual firm rather than of the total industry ( profits) hangs as a Damoclean sword over the industry: price-cutting warfare may break out. In the words of the same corporation official last quoted:

> And when I call a guy a dirty, low kind of a so-and-so price cutter, he knows he has been called a price cutter. . . . I would tell him further that if he didn't stop these damn price cuttings, I would show him how to cut prices, and many times I did cut them, and when I cut a price, and if it was your price I was cutting, take it from me, brother, you knew your price had been cut.[12]

The firms in the industry would rather see the hair which mythology tells us held up the sword replaced by a good strong rope. This is the advantage of agreement. But the rope of agreement has its own weak strands, for agreements, being illegal, cannot be enforced in the courts.

## PRICE UNIFORMITY

When prices of all sellers in the marketplace at any one moment of time are uniform, this may be evidence of one of three possible situations. The first is that where there are many buyers and sellers who have good knowledge of the market alternatives, there appears to be no one firm which stands out prominently in the marketplace, and price is determined by impersonal market forces. As a result, all sellers charge the same price. In the second situation there are relatively few sellers, and they believe that the price charged by one of the firms, usually the largest, is a fair price and independently decide to follow that price. This is the case of "price leadership." The effectiveness of leadership in establishing uniform prices will depend a good deal upon how

[12] *Ibid.*

many small sellers there are on the periphery of this oligopoly and the degree of product differentiation. The more small sellers there are, the greater will be the instability of price. The greater the differentiation of product, the less will the sellers be able to find a peg upon which to hang a given price. In the third situation, a similar market structure exists, but the sellers have conspired not to compete in terms of price. Although prices are uniform in all three cases, the pricing is illegal only under the third possibility. The fact that prices are identical in itself proves nothing. A conspiracy must be demonstrated to exist.

In the first case, a conspiracy to fix prices is impossible because there are too many sellers; it may be difficult enough for even a very few sellers to settle upon acceptable terms of an agreement. The only way that an agreement can be reached where there are many sellers is to have the government support the endeavor. Thus farmers, through the passage of the Capper-Volstead Act of 1922, are permitted to act together in associations to process and market their goods. But this type of case does not concern us here.

It is the differences between the second and third cases which arouse most discussion and litigation, for the market structure may be identical in both cases. The follower may follow the price of the "price leader" because he wants to, not necessarily because there is an agreement; this is one of the freedoms the follower has under the free enterprise system. Published price lists may facilitate such leader and followership. Actually, the so-called price leader may be desirous of discarding the cloak of leadership; but this may not be easily accomplished, for other sellers may look to him as a "reference seller." On the other side of the coin, small sellers may be afraid not to follow the leader's price for fear that a price cut will invite predatory retaliation which will drive the price down to the point where the small firm cannot survive. In any case, the symptoms of strong price leadership are the same as those of a collusive agreement: all sellers charge the same price. There must be, then, strong evidence of an agreement if a charge of price-fixing is to hold up. But price leadership in itself is not illegal.[13]

---

[13] *United States v. International Harvester Co.*, 274 U.S. 693 (1927).

The best evidence to prove collusion is to have witnesses who will readily testify about the time and place and terms of the agreement. An initial witness may implicate others. If the government agrees, a witness may be granted immunity against prosecution if he testifies against his colleagues. And as more become implicated, more testify. This is what occurred in the electrical equipment industry price-fixing cases of 1960. Other evidence may be correspondence, but evidence so incriminating is likely to be destroyed or sent to residential rather than business addresses without any identification of the senders. Such written correspondence is unlikely, therefore, to be obtained.

Trade associations have been frequently involved in price-fixing schemes, probably largely because they provide a central meeting place and their activities may sometimes become effective implementing devices for pricing agreements. The principal functions of the trade association are to provide better information on industry conditions to its members, to supply nationwide sales promotion programs, and even to finance or conduct basic research. The information disseminated may concern costs, credit data, labor relations, industry capacity, and similar facts, including prices, which presumably will enable the individual competitors to operate in a more economic fashion. The danger here is that some of these data may become the basis for a price conspiracy. Are price data being distributed in order to indicate what prices have been in the past,[14] or are they being reported in order to provide the members with knowledge of what they should be now or in the immediate future as part of a price-fixing scheme?[15] The legality of a price-reporting system will depend upon the inference drawn from it by the courts. This same principle applies to any statistical data distributed to members by a trade association: if the inference is warranted that such data are the implementing device behind a price-fixing arrangement, then their distribution is illegal.

Basing-point pricing by the members of an industry is illegal because it represents a systematic method of pricing. Each seller knows exactly what price will be charged by his competitors to a

[14] *Maple Flooring Mfrs. Association v. United States,* 268 U.S. 563 (1925).
[15] *Sugar Institute, Inc. v. United States,* 297 U.S. 553 (1936).

customer at any location in the United States because he can apply a simple formula. Delivered prices are quoted to customers by taking the lowest sum of any base price plus rail transportation from that base. As long as a seller knows what the prices are at the base points and also what the standard shipping rates are, he can calculate the delivered price which the other members of the group will be quoting to the customer. The result: a buyer will be quoted the same delivered price by all sellers. Thus it was that substantially the whole cement industry was found guilty of a price-fixing conspiracy under Section 5 of the Federal Trade Commission Act because the cement firms, with the aid of their trade association, which distributed the same railroad freight-rate books to all its members, were quoting identical delivered prices.[16] The fact that the cement companies refused to ship by any other means than rail provided the clincher. Similarly, a zone system of pricing, under which identical prices are quoted by all sellers to the buyers within a geographical zone, is illegal.[17]

Quoting the same delivered price that another seller quotes does not mean, however, that that price is necessarily collusively determined. A firm may be simply meeting the competition of a rival's price which is lower than the firm's own f.o.b. price plus freight from its own plant. This meeting of a competitor's price may be done legally on a sporadic basis, for this would seem to indicate that it is being done as a competitive, rather than a collusive, act. But if it were being done on a regular basis, the price would be suspect of being collusively determined.

Evidence of concert of action does not have to be express. It can be implied from the business behavior, from the "conscious parallelism of action." When several distributors and exhibitors of motion picture films adopted like price schedules for first-run theaters and for subsequent runs which represented a drastic change from the previous practice, the court came to only one conclusion:

It taxes credulity to believe that the several distributors would, in the

[16] *Federal Trade Commission v. Cement Institute,* 333 U.S. 683 (1948).
[17] *Chain Institute, Inc. v. Federal Trade Commission,* 246 F.2d 231 (1957), *cert. denied,* 355 U.S. 895 (1957).

circumstances, have accepted and put into operation with substantial unanimity such far-reaching changes in their business methods without some understanding that all were to join, and we reject as beyond the range of probability that it was the result of mere chance.[18]

And when the Army Engineers opened eleven sealed bids on the procurement of 6,000 barrels of cement and found all eleven quoting a figure of $3.28654 per barrel, no wonder collusion was suspected. A court of appeals failed to uphold a Federal Trade Commission order against the sellers, but a dissenting judge, later upheld in his position by the Supreme Court, commented:

> Conspiracies are usually established by circumstantial evidence. Seldom do the offenders make solemn written agreements. While circumstantial evidence may be less persuasive in some cases, it by no means follows that it is necessarily weak or lacking in conviction carrying-power.[19]

It should be emphasized, however, that conscious parallelism of action is not enough to condemn. In the words of Justice Clark in a 1954 decision:

> This Court has never held that proof of parallel business behavior conclusively establishes agreement or, phrased differently, that such behavior itself constitutes a Sherman Act offense. Circumstantial evidence of consciously parallel behavior may have made heavy inroads into the traditional judicial attitude toward conspiracy; but "conscious parallelism" has not yet read conspiracy out of the Sherman Act entirely.[20]

Even in the matter of sealed bids, different reasons may help account for identical bidding. The Attorney General observed in 1962 with respect to identical bids received in public procurement:

> The diverse factors which may be responsible for identical bidding suggests that a case-by-case approach is essential to determine the underlying factors responsible for such bidding. . . .
> Effective utilization of identical bidding reports requires that they be buttressed by economic and legal inquiries to determine, (a) the demand characteristics of the product, (b) the structure of the market, (c) the factors

---

[18] *Interstate Circuit, Inc. v. United States,* 306 U.S. 208, 223 (1939).

[19] *Aetna Portland Cement Co. v. Federal Trade Commission,* 157 F.2d 533, 576–577 (1946) ; *reversed,* 333 U.S. 683 (1948) .

[20] *Theatre Enterprises, Inc. v. Paramount Film Distributing Corp.,* 346 U.S. 537, 540 (1954).

influencing the observed price behavior, and (d) the antitrust implications of these economic factors.[21]

## NONIDENTICAL BIDDING

We have stressed the fact that price uniformity may be a symptom of collusion where the sellers are few. But this does not necessarily mean that if, for example, all sealed bids show different figures, there has not been collusion. In the 1960 electrical equipment industry price-fixing cases the defendants used a formula designated as "phase of the moon." Through cyclic rotating positioning inherent in the formula, the sellers took turns quoting low price, intermediate price, and high price. Under this system each seller received his share of the business at a noncompetitive price. In view of the fact that uniformity of price is often highly suspect where there are few sellers in the market and might well be considered circumstantial evidence, the chances are great that sellers would prefer, in a price agreement, to use such cyclic rotation.

Cyclic rotation in the bidding process need not, of course, be the result of agreement. Different prices may be due simply to differences in cost calculations and profit expectations. And the sellers can be well aware that the successful bids are being rotated. The sellers can allocate the business among themselves by observing which rivals were the low bidders in the previous bidding and which competitors have the largest shop load. It may well be that some of the bidders do not actually want the business, but submit "courtesy bids," which in some instances at least will provide a minimum number of bids and ensure that all bids will not be rejected for lack of a sufficient number. Such behavior is unlikely, however, unless the industry is operating at close to full capacity; and it is in times of excess capacity that the danger of price-cutting is greatest. Such conscious cyclic rotation without agreement also requires a tight oligopoly where

[21] Report of the Attorney General under Executive Order 10936, *Identical Bidding in Public Procurement,* pp. 28–29. The Executive Order, dated Apr. 24, 1961 (26 Fed. Reg. 3555), requires that all departments, agencies, and instrumentalities of the Federal government transmit to the Attorney General reports of identical bids submitted in advertised procurement of property or services exceeding $10,000 in total amount.

there are so few sellers that recalcitrant conduct is not to be expected.

## COSTS OF CONSPIRACY

The costs of being found guilty of charges of price-fixing can be high. The greatest money cost is likely to be that paid under private civil treble-damage suits filed by past customers who have paid the rigged prices. Such suits, supported by the prima facie evidence of the conviction for price-fixing, can bring those filing suit three times the value of the overcharge. How much the overcharge has been is a matter to be worked out between the litigants either through court procedures or out-of-court agreement. In the electrical equipment industry cases more than 1,800 suits for damages were brought. General Electric Company estimated that total settlements with customers would exceed $160 million.[22]

A violation of the Sherman Act is a misdemeanor. A corporation can thus be fined up to $50,000 for each violation of which it is found guilty, and corporate employees can be fined $50,000 and/or imprisoned for up to one year. In the twenty electrical equipment industry price-fixing conspiracy cases, fines totaling almost $2 million were imposed in 1961 on twenty-nine corporations and forty-five company officials. Total corporate fines were $1,787,000. The fines of the individual officers were around $2,000 or $3,000, although one defendant was fined $12,500. Seven corporate officials were sentenced to thirty days in prison. Judge Ganey imposed these prison sentences (which previously had been almost unheard of) and relatively heavy fines because he was much concerned with the implications that these conspiracies bore for both the economy and the modern corporation. In his own words:

> This is a shocking indictment of a vast section of our economy, for what is really at stake here is the survival of the kind of economy under which America has grown to greatness, the free enterprise system.
>
> The conduct of the corporate and individual defendants alike, in the words of the distinguished assistant attorney general who headed the Antitrust Division of the Department of Justice have flagrantly mocked the image of that economic system of free enterprise which we profess to the country....

[22] *The Wall Street Journal,* Apr. 30, 1964, p. 4.

One would be most naïve indeed to believe that these violations of the law, so long persisted in, affecting so large a segment of the industry and finally, involving so many millions upon millions of dollars, were facts unknown to those responsible for the conduct of the corporation. . . .

I [am] convinced that in the great number of these defendants' cases, they were torn between conscience and an approved corporate policy, with the rewarding objectives of promotion, comfortable security and large salaries —in short, the organization or the company man, the conformist, who goes along with his superiors and finds balm for his conscience in additional comforts and the security of his place in the corporate set-up.[23]

The top management of the two largest corporations involved in the 1960 price-fixing cases, General Electric Company and Westinghouse Electric Corporation, have denied knowledge of the price-fixing activities of the corporations' executives who were so engaged. What they did not deny was that safeguards to prevent such illegal activity by subordinates had been inadequate. General Electric Company's directive policy 20.5, issued in 1954, was perfectly clear and stated, in part:

It is the policy of the company to comply strictly with the antitrust laws. There shall be no exception to this policy nor shall it be compromised or qualified by anyone acting for or on behalf of the company. No employee shall enter into any understanding, agreement, plan, or scheme, expressed or implied, formal or informal, with any competitor, in regard to prices, terms, or conditions of sale, production, distribution, territories, or customers; nor exchange or discuss with a competitor prices, terms, or conditons of sale or any other competitive information; nor engage in any other conduct which in the opinion of the company's counsel violates any of the antitrust laws.[24]

But such a directive obviously had not been successful in preventing company officials from working out price-fixing agreements as a means of dealing with deep price-cutting (as much as 45 per cent off list price in 1954–1955).

The principal corporations involved in this price-fixing have found it necessary, therefore, to build into the corporation safeguards not only to protect it from renewed antitrust assault but also to preserve its own integrity as a valid part of the free enterprise system and to create a favorable corporate image in the

[23] *The New York Times*, Feb. 7, 1961, p. 26.

[24] *Administered Prices, Hearings before the Subcommittee on Antitrust and Monopoly of the Senate Committee on the Judiciary*, 87th Cong., 1st Sess., 1961, part 27, p. 17120.

eyes of the public. Educational programs on pricing and the marketing responsibilities of company employees have been inaugurated. Legal departments have been strengthened, placing new emphasis on antitrust and the function of educating employees. New financial auditing techniques have been adopted to identify possible illegal pricing. A group of specially designated outside advisors has recommended to one of these corporations that a program of continuing economic and legal education for its managerial and sales personnel be conducted.[25]

## FAIR TRADE LEGISLATION

Under state fair trade acts a producer or distributor of a good bearing his brand, trademark, or name can prescribe by contract either a minimum or a stipulated resale price of that good, depending upon the particular state law. Prior to the passage of the fair trade laws, resale price maintenance agreements were considered illegal because such agreements by a producer with more than one distributor prevent price competition among those distributors.[26] The effect is the same as if the distributors had combined and agreed to fix price.

In late 1963 forty states had fair trade laws; of these, twenty-three had "nonsigner" clauses.[27] According to the nonsigner provision, all resellers are bound by the terms of the resale price maintenance contract signed by any *one* reseller. To be truly effective, a state fair trade law must contain a nonsigner provision; for unless the manufacturer has some control over the noncontracting price-cutter, there can be little effective control by the manufacturer over resale prices. In addition, in late 1963 special legislation in nine states made resale price maintenance with respect to alcoholic beverages either mandatory or subject to control by state liquor control agencies.

[25] *A Report from the Board of Advice to Westinghouse Electric Corporation,* July, 1962, p. 11. The Board consisted of Dean Erwin N. Griswold of the Harvard Law School, Dean Eugene V. Rostow of the Yale Law School, Prof. S. Chesterfield Oppenheim of Michigan Law School, and Dr. A. D. H. Kaplan of the Brookings Institution.

[26] *Dr. Miles Medical Co. v. John D. Park & Sons Co.,* 220 U.S. 373 (1911).

[27] Fair trade laws or nonsigner clauses thereof which have been declared unconstitutional by a state's highest court are not included in these figures even though they may not have been repealed.

Not all branded goods are covered by the fair trade laws. Closeout sales are excepted. Exceptions are made in some of these laws on sales to colleges and libraries. Some make provisions to except damaged goods or those from which the brand or trade names have been removed or obliterated.

The state of California, in 1931, was the first state to adopt fair trade legislation. The Supreme Court, in a 1936 decision, approved of state fair trade, including the nonsigner clause.[28] State fair trade laws are only applicable to the commerce within the relevant state. But Federal enabling legislation has been passed for the purpose of exempting from the Federal antitrust laws resale price maintenance contracts under state fair trade acts with respect to goods sold in interstate commerce. The Miller-Tydings Resale Price Maintenance Act of 1937 amended Section 1 of the Sherman Act to exempt this type of vertical price-fixing from the antitrust laws, making it applicable to the Federal Trade Commission Act as well. And in 1952, after the Supreme Court found that the Miller-Tydings Act did not apply to the nonsigner provisions of state laws,[29] Section 5 of the Federal Trade Commission Act was amended by the McGuire-Keogh Fair Trade Enabling Act to include in this exemption the nonsigner provision. This amendment was made applicable to any of the Federal antitrust acts and extended the coverage to stipulated as well as minimum prices. The constitutionality of the McGuire-Keogh Act has been upheld by a court of appeals,[30] and the Supreme Court refused to review that decision.[31] This does not mean that a state court cannot find a nonsigner provision of a state fair trade act unconstitutional. Indeed, the fact that only twenty-three of the forty state fair trade laws have nonsigner provisions still considered constitutional is a clear measure of the degree to which this has occurred. It simply means that nonsigner provisions cannot be deemed unlawful under the Federal antitrust laws.

An obstacle to the success of fair trade is the fact that cut-

[28] *Old Dearborn Distributing Co. v. Seagram Distillers Corp.*, 299 U.S. 183 (1936).

[29] *Schwegmann Bros. v. Calvert Distillers Corp.*, 341 U.S. 384 (1951).

[30] *Eli Lilly & Co. v. Schwegmann Bros.*, 205 F.2d 788 (1953).

[31] 346 U.S. 856 (1953).

price mail-order shipments of goods out of an area which has no fair trade law into a fair-trade state cannot be prevented by an enforcement action under the fair trade law of the state into which the goods are shipped. For the buyer takes title to the goods in the location from which the goods are shipped.[32] The mail-order business can thus be used to evade a state fair trade act. Likewise, an advertisement within a fair-trade state of cut prices on goods available in a non-fair-trade area has been judged not to be within the jurisdiction of the state fair trade law.[33] Sales from within a fair-trade state to customers outside the state in a non-fair-trade area cannot, however, be made at cut prices.

Maintaining a fair-trade program is fraught with several legal problems. Responsibility for enforcement falls upon the producer or distributor, who must monitor and take legal action against the price-cutters. Legal enforcement must be continuous, vigorous, and effective; it cannot be selective. An assortment of marketing devices contrived by retailers to evade fair-trade prices, such as the granting of trading stamps in abnormally high volume or the placing of excessive value on the trade-in of durable consumer items, must be dealt with by court action. Further, utilization of fair trade prevents a manufacturer from itself selling in competition with those distributors, either wholesalers or retailers, who are governed by its fair-trade contracts, for the effect of such an arrangement is a horizontal agreement.

If the producer does not choose to avail himself of the privilege available under a fair trade law, then a recourse available to the producer in an effort to ensure resale price maintenance is to refuse to deal with those resellers who will not maintain the resale prices at the level desired by the producer. This is the so-called "Colgate doctrine."[34] This action on the part of the producer must be strictly unilateral, however. There can be no agreement whatsoever, whether express or implied.[35] Attempts by fair-trade sellers to prevent retail price-cutting by discussing

[32] *General Electric Co. v. Masters Mail Order Co.*, 244 F.2d 681 (1957), *cert. denied*, 355 U.S. 824 (1957).

[33] *Bissell Carpet Sweeper Co. v. Masters Mail Order Co. of Washington, D.C., Inc.*, 240 F.2d 684 (1957).

[34] *United States v. Colgate & Co.*, 250 U.S. 300 (1919).

[35] *United States v. A. Schrader's Son, Inc.*, 252 U.S. 85 (1920).

the retail price situation with competing retailers or by inducing wholesalers to refuse to do business with price-cutting retailers amount to combinations or agreements in violation of the Sherman Act.[36]

## FAIR TRADE AND COMPETITION

Retailers have urged the passage of fair trade legislation and have exhorted manufacturers to make use of resale price maintenance on the grounds that it protects the retailer from the selective price-cutting known as loss-leader selling. This selling practice occurs when a particular item is singled out by a seller to be sold at a very attractive low price to induce consumers to enter the store where they will purchase other goods as well at prices yielding a normal or perhaps a larger-than-normal margin of profit. Typically this item is a well-known branded good with a price that is usually known by the average consumer. Advertising such a product at a lower price is, therefore, a real attraction. This price may even be below invoice cost to the retailer. Actually it may be but a matter of not yielding to the retailer his normal margin on this item. In any case, the smaller retailer, forced to meet this competition, considers this pricing action destructive to his profits. If it is carried far enough, he may be forced out of business. It is thus that it is sometimes designated "predatory" price-cutting. A true predatory price competition involves an intent to destroy the competitor. Such intent is difficult to prove, for any competition presumably involves a desire to best the competitor in sales.

Discount houses and chain stores, marketing institutions which generally attempt to compete on the basis of lower prices and relatively large volume, are usually cited as being the most prevalent users of loss-leader selling tactics. To these marketers the loss leader is usually but one factor contributing to increased turnover. Losses in the aggregate for such stores are not necessarily incurred. The overhead costs are simply being spread over a larger number of units sold. The average (per unit) total costs are being covered by price. It is not difficult, however, to understand why the small retailer, doing a relatively small volume of

[36] *United States v. Parke, Davis & Co.*, 362 U.S. 29 (1960).

business and frequently dealing in a smaller number of items, objects to this form of price competition. For the position of this so-called family retailer is being threatened by the encroachments and sales tactics of the larger, more impersonal, marketing outlets.

It is also argued that the manufacturer has a stake in maintaining resale prices. If a particular branded product is used as a loss leader, the price-cutting of this product will become general and, in the mind of the consumer, the true value of the product will be lost. An accompanying argument is that as the margin of profit on the branded goods in question is no longer satisfactory to the dealers, they will no longer be interested in selling these products.

The right of the manufacturer of branded merchandise to control by contract the resale prices of his goods is supported at law, in essence, by this very argument. This is known as the goodwill theory of fair trade and was at the heart of the Supreme Court's acceptance of fair trade in its 1936 decision. Manufacturers, when they advertise their brand names, are making an investment in goodwill. This goodwill represents a property value which belongs to the manufacturer. When the latter sells his branded goods to distributors, he retains the goodwill although parting with the physical good itself. Therefore, as long as that brand name is attached to the product, the manufacturer has the legal right, by controlling the resale price, to protect the value of this property right. By the same token, if the name or mark is removed from the good so that the seller cannot capitalize on the goodwill, then the reseller can sell it at a price of his own choosing. Fair trade legislation, under this thinking, is an appropriate exercise of the state's police power to protect this property right.

The proponents of fair trade argue that the consumer also suffers from loss-leader selling. Logically, it would seem that the lower the price of the loss leader, all other things being equal, the greater the benefit to the consumer. But, goes the argument, the consumer may lose because all other things are not equal; that is, the prices of other goods in the same store have been marked up. In other words, this argument proposes that fixed retail prices will prevent deceptive pricing. A further argument in behalf of fixed retail prices is that no time need be wasted by the consumer higgling over prices. This argument clearly assumes that the consumer does not wish to seek price bargains.

The basic argument against resale price maintenance is that it prevents the full operation of price competition. Prices and the price system, according to the economist, form the basic mechanism which allocates resources with the best results for society. Fair trade introduces a certain amount of rigidity into the price mechanism. As a result, the most efficient economic units are not always the only ones to survive, prices are higher than they otherwise would be, and excess capacity will exist. For these reasons the Federal Trade Commission, the Antitrust Division of the Department of Justice, and most economists have argued quite consistently against fair trade. They view the fair trade laws as exemptions to antitrust which are not economically justified. The value of a producer's goodwill and brand name should be determined by the marketplace, and the laws of antitrust and unfair competition can guard against predatory pricing tactics.

### STATE SALES-BELOW-COST LAWS

Supplementing the fair trade laws are state sales-below-cost or minimum markup laws, which apply to all goods, branded or unbranded. They *require,* with qualification, that prices cover cost. "Cost" is usually defined in such a way as to cover invoice or replacement cost, whichever is lower, plus a markup to cover costs of operation including overhead. These laws thus are intended to prevent cut-price selling. Known on the statute books as unfair sales or unfair trade practices acts, these state sales-below-cost laws are worded to proclaim against sales below cost in order to prevent unfair injury to competitors, deception of the public, and monopoly.

Thirty-one states have passed general sales-below-cost laws. The depression conditions of the 1930s stimulated their passage. Of the twenty-eight still considered constitutional in late 1963, half specified a minimum markup for wholesalers, usually of 2 per cent. For retailers, nineteen of these laws required markups of from 4 to 12 per cent; but there was only one at 12 per cent, and most specified 6 per cent. Where percentage markups are not specified, the markup must cover the "cost of doing business," which is defined differently as to detail in the several acts. But "cost of doing business" is supposed to cover *all* costs, and some state laws specifically include labor, executive salaries, rent, interest on borrowed capital, depreciation, selling cost, maintenance of equipment, credit losses, license fees, taxes, insurance, and advertising. In some states, where a trade association has an established cost survey for the locality in question, these cost data may be used as competent evidence in litigation. Manufacturers are subject to this type of law in twelve states. Only ten such laws apply to the service trades.

In addition to the state sales-below-cost laws of general application, twenty-seven states had, in late 1963, sales-below-cost laws (still considered constitutional) applying to *specific* goods. The principal commodities represented by such laws were cigarettes, milk and dairy products, and gasoline.

Certain types of sales are exempt from the minimum markup laws, although those which are exempt will vary from state to state. Usually exempted are sales made for charitable purposes or to relief agencies, clearance and closeout sales, sales made under court order, sales involving the liquidation of a business, and sales of perishable, seasonal, damaged, or deteriorated goods.

The state minimum markup laws do not make sales-below-cost illegal per se. They declare it unlawful to advertise, offer to sell, or sell goods below cost only where the intent, or the effect, is to injure competitors and destroy competition. The general assumption of these laws is that injury to a competitor is synonymous with injury to competition. Thus where the law uses the word "effect," a diversion of sales from one seller to another as a result of cut-price sales may be enough to constitute a violation of the law. Where intent must be shown, a distinction has to be made between ordinary price competition and intentionally destructive price-cutting. In some of these laws a sale below cost is prima facie evidence of intent to injure competition. Here the wording of a state law is crucial as to what constitutes statutory presumptions, prima facie evidence, and necessary evidence or proof.

The sales-below-cost laws of all but three states permit selling below cost if done in good faith to meet the price of a competitor. This proviso applies generally to similar or comparable, but not necessarily to identical, products. Whether the competitor's price which is being met must be a legal price, what constitutes an unlawful price of a competitor, and the standards to be used to measure the legality of such a price vary among the several state laws.

The indirect methods of price competition which can be employed without coming in conflict with the minimum markup laws again depend upon the particular law and its interpretations by the courts. The legality of the giving away of free merchandise, of the selling of two or more goods in combination at a single price, or of the giving of prizes or premiums will depend primarily on their intent or their effect. Trading stamps are mentioned specifically in some of the sales-below-cost laws, but are usually permitted if they do not represent below-cost selling. Some states have treated the giving of trading stamps as a cash discount for the prompt payment of cash. Such a cash discount does not represent a lower price that can then be treated as a price cut which can be met directly by the competitor.[37] When trading stamps are given in larger amounts than might be assumed to be a customary cash discount or when they are redeemable at values exceeding such customary level, they may be violative of the law.

Trading stamps as a method of competition have been singled out for special legislative treatment by several of the states. The Supreme Court held in 1916 that it is within the police power of the state to prohibit the use of trading stamps.[38] But only one state, Kansas, prohibits their use. Seven states have regulated the use of trading stamps in terms of requiring that redemption be made available in cash as an alternative to merchandise premiums. By and large, the attempts to regulate trading-stamp activity have been unsuccessful. Trading stamps

[37] The United States Supreme Court, in ruling the Oklahoma Unfair Sales Act constitutional, accepted the concept of the trading stamp as a cash discount. *Safeway Stores, Inc. v. Oklahoma Retail Grocers Association, Inc.*, 360 U.S. 334 (1959).

[38] *Rast v. Van Deman & Lewis*, 240 U.S. 342; *Tanner v. Little*, 240 U.S. 369; and *Pitney v. Washington*, 240 U.S. 387 (1916).

have not come under the prohibition of state gift enterprise statutes because they have not been deemed to contain an element of chance. The Federal Trade Commission has taken the position that trading-stamp plans in themselves are not an unfair method of competition.[39]

Enforcement of sales-below-cost laws can generally be accomplished through litigation brought by either private or public parties. Suits can be for damages, for an injunction, or, where by an arm of the government, for the imposition of fines or imprisonment. Twelve states specifically permit trade associations to bring suit, but efforts in concert by groups of competitors to enforce these laws have been halted, through consent decrees, as being in violation of the Sherman Act. In most of the states no administrative agency has been established with the special responsibility of administering or enforcing the sales-below-cost law. Litigation has not been as frequent as it has been for fair trade because the markups provided for have not been as large, the vested interests concerned with the desire to enforce have not been as directly related to or as responsible for preventing the price-cutting, and qualifications such as "good-faith meeting of competition" or "intent to destroy a competitor" are written into the laws themselves.

### SUGGESTIONS FOR FURTHER READING

For analysis of collusive price behavior and/or its symptoms, see John A. Howard, "Collusive Behavior," *Journal of Business,* July, 1954; John Q. Lawyer, "How to Conspire to Fix Prices," *Harvard Business Review,* March–April, 1963; "The Anatomy of a Price-fixing Conspiracy," *Business Week,* Sept. 8, 1962, pp. 72–73; Vernon A. Mund, "Identical Bid Prices," *Journal of Political Economy,* April, 1960; and Paul W. Cook, Jr., "Fact and Fancy in Identical Bids," *Harvard Business Review,* January–February, 1963. The best explanation of systematic basing-point pricing is by Fritz Machlup, *The Basing Point System,* McGraw-Hill Book Company, New York, 1949.

What went on inside the electrical equipment industry price conspiracies is described by Richard A. Smith in "The Incredible Electrical Conspiracy," part I, *Fortune,* April, 1961; how the Department of Justice broke the case is described in part II, May, 1961. The part in the conspiracy played by the individual corporation executives as portrayed by their own testimony, as

[39] Federal Trade Commission press release, Oct. 3, 1957.

well as exhibits in the case, are presented in *Administered Prices, Hearings before the Subcommittee on Antitrust and Monopoly of the Senate Committee on the Judiciary,* parts 27 and 28, "Price Fixing and Bid Rigging in the Electrical Manufacturing Industry," 87th Cong., 1st Sess., 1961. A journalistic version of the conspiracy is that of John G. Fuller, *The Gentlemen Conspirators,* Grove Press, Inc., New York, 1962.

The legal position of the trade association is presented in G. P. Lamb and S. S. Kittelle, *Trade Association Law and Practice,* Oppenheim Trade Regulation Series, Little, Brown and Company, Boston, 1956. A shorter analysis is that of J. S. Hays and J. L. Ratzkin, "Trade Association Practices and Antitrust Law," *Harvard Business Review,* Summer, 1947.

The most complete studies of fair trade are by the Federal Trade Commission, *Report on Resale Price Maintenance,* Washington, 1945; and by the House Committee on Small Business, *Fair Trade: The Problem and the Issues,* H. Rept. 1292, 82d Cong., 2d Sess., 1952.

Discussion of minimum markup laws can be found in Robert Tannenbaum, "Cost under the Unfair Practices Acts," in *Studies in Business Administration,* vol. IX, no. 2, University of Chicago Press, Chicago, 1939; and Richard H. Lovell (Comment), "Sales below Cost Prohibitions: Private Price Fixing under State Law," *Yale Law Journal,* January, 1948. An excellent study which points up the confusion which exists between loss-leader selling and active price competition is the *Report on an Inquiry into Loss-leader, Selling,* prepared by the Restrictive Trade Practices Commission, Ottawa, Canada, 1955.

# 3

# *PRICE DISCOUNTS*

Sellers, in making sales to business customers, do not always charge the same prices. Price discounts to particular buyers may be based on the fact that those buyers buy in large quantities (quantity discounts). Lower prices may be granted to wholesalers than to retailers for the same volume of goods (functional discounts). Lower prices to some buyers may be granted on the basis of clearance of perishable or obsolete goods. Sellers may charge lower prices to particular buyers in order to hold them as customers or to procure them as new customers ("meeting the competition"). A financially powerful seller may favor customers in a particular geographic market with the objective of driving competitors from that market (predatory geographic price discrimination). Allowances granted by a seller to a buyer for advertising and promotion services provided by the buyer in connection with the resale of the seller's goods may be equivalent to a reduction in the price of those goods to some of the buyers if such allowances are not made available to all the buyers on the same basic terms. Conversely, a seller who provides buyers with services or facilities for promoting the resale of the seller's goods may not always do so for all buyers on the same terms.

The laws which deal most directly with these differences in prices are known as the "price discrimination" laws. Their principal objective is to prohibit those price differences which injure competition or prevent competition with any person or firm. This is not an easy task, for price differences based on differences in economic efficiency must be distinguished from those which result solely from differences in bargaining power. The former are usually referred to as "price differentials," the latter as "price discriminations." But not all price discriminations are illegal. The price discrimination laws generally condemn only those price discriminations which might injure competition substantially, prevent competition with any person, or tend to create a monopoly. The wording of the statutes and the efforts of the administrators of the law to achieve equity both for the competitor and in the competition leave much to be desired, as we shall see in this chapter.

## LEGISLATION AGAINST PRICE DISCRIMINATION

Price discrimination is specifically mentioned in legislation in one way or another in every state of the union. In some states the practice is singled out for special legislation, which may be directed against the practice in general or against the practice in certain industries, such as those involving dairy products, alcoholic beverages, insurance, and petroleum products. In other states coverage of price discrimination is included within the statutes against monopolies and restraints of trade. The discriminations declared illegal are those which are "unfair," those which destroy or prevent the competition of any person or business, those which have the purpose or effect of destroying or substantially lessening or preventing competition, or those tending to create a monopoly. As with much other state trade regulation, enforcement of such laws is not extensive.

The Federal law specifically designed to control price discrimination is the Robinson-Patman Act of 1936, which amended Section 2 of the Clayton Act of 1914. Section 3 of the Robinson-Patman Act also attacks price discrimination, making it illegal to discriminate against competitors of a purchaser, to sell at prices lower in one part of the country than those elsewhere in the country, or to sell goods at "unreasonably low prices" for the purpose of destroying competition or eliminating a competitor. But Section 3 is a criminal statute outside the jurisdiction of the Federal Trade Commission and cannot be used as the basis for private treble-damage actions because it is technically not a part of the antitrust laws,[1] and as a result it has lain largely dormant. Discrimination in price can also be attacked under the Sherman Act when such market conduct becomes a monopolistic restraint of trade. And Section 5 of the Federal Trade Commission Act can attack the practice as an unfair method of competition. Finally, with respect to imported goods, the Revenue Act of 1916 makes it unlawful to sell them at a price substantially less than actual market value or wholesale price where the intent is to injure or destroy an industry in the United States.

When granting lower prices to some buyers, marketers must be principally concerned and fully conversant with the amended Section 2 provisions of the Clayton Act. Applying to interstate commerce, this statute is actively enforced by the Federal Trade Commission. Because the Robinson-Patman Act is the principal law with which businessmen must contend with respect to price discrimination, we shall confine our detailed analysis in this chapter to its provisions.

### SECTION 2 PROVISIONS OF THE ROBINSON-PATMAN ACT[2]

The Robinson-Patman Act does not make "price discrimination" illegal per se. Section 2(a), applying to goods of "like grade and quality," declares price discrimination to be unlawful only "where the effect of such discrimination may be substantially to lessen competition or tend to create a monopoly in any line of commerce, or to injure, destroy, or prevent competition with any person who either grants or knowingly receives the benefit of such discrimination, or with customers of either of them." The applicability of the law to price discrimination is thus qualified by use of such undefined words as "may," "substantially," "lessen," and "tend." This section also permits price differentials where there is "only due allowance for differences in the cost of

---

[1] *Nashville Milk Co. v. Carnation Co.*, 355 U.S. 373, and *Safeway Stores, Inc. v. Vance*, 355 U.S. 389 (1958). The constitutionality of Section 3 of the Robinson-Patman Act was upheld in *United States v. National Dairy Products Corp.*, 372 U.S. 29 (1963).

[2] Technically, the references to Section 2 are to Section 2 of the amended Clayton Act and not to Section 2 of the Robinson-Patman Act. See Appendix B for the full wording of the amended Section 2 of the Clayton Act.

manufacture, sale, or delivery resulting from the differing methods or quantities in which such commodities are to such purchasers sold or delivered." Also allowed for are changing market conditions which may affect the marketability of goods, such as deterioration of perishable goods, obsolescence of seasonal goods, distress sales under court process, or sales made during a good faith discontinuance of a business. These are all provisions of Section 2(*a*). It may also be noted that this section contains a provision that nothing in the act shall prevent sellers from selecting their own customers as long as this is not in restraint of trade.

Section 2(*b*) permits a seller to discriminate in price "in good faith to meet an equally low price of a competitor, or the services or facilities furnished by a competitor." Exactly what constitutes "good faith" is a much-argued matter and will be explored later in this chapter.

In spite of these exemptions, the Robinson-Patman Act makes a detailed effort to control price discrimination. Section 2(*f*) makes it unlawful knowingly to receive as well as to induce a discrimination in price. Indirect means of price discrimination are likewise banned in the act. To pay a customer for services or facilities furnished by the customer in connection with the processing, handling, sale, or offer to sell of the seller's goods is unlawful unless such a payment is made "available on proportionally equal terms" to all other competing customers [Section 2(*d*)]. Similarly, the law insists that any services or facilities furnished to the customer by the seller to aid the customer in his handling or marketing of the seller's goods be likewise made available to all buyers on "proportionally equal terms" [Section 2(*e*)]. But proportional *to what* is not stated in either instance.

Two additional provisions of the act have been highly controversial because their economic justification is in doubt. The first is the provision within Section 2(*a*) permitting the Federal Trade Commission to fix and establish for particular commodities or classes of commodities quantity limits "where it finds that available purchasers in greater quantities are so few as to render differentials on account thereof unjustly discriminatory or promotive of monopoly." Whereas the objective of preventing monopoly is legitimate, economies of scale may be denied their proper dues. The second is Section 2(*c*), which requires that no discounts in the nature of brokerage payments be made except to intermediaries who are entirely independent of the buyer and the seller. This provision is intended to prevent a large firm from demanding a discount in the name of "brokerage," but it also denies a firm the right to be rewarded for performing the function of a broker.

## PRICE DISCRIMINATION AND THE LEVEL OF COMPETITION

Essentially, three levels of competition may be substantially lessened or injured by price discrimination under the terms of the Robinson-Patman Act. One is that between the two sellers at what may be called the primary level of competition. Seller A may sell at lower prices than seller B in a particular geographic market, holding up his prices elsewhere, with the eventual result that seller B loses sales and may, in the long run, be forced out of business. A bakery operating in interstate commerce cut the wholesale price of its bread in one town but not in any other town or state, forcing a local baker out of business. The discrimination was between the buyers in that one town on the one hand and the buyers in all the other towns on the other hand. But the injury was to the baker, or the seller, in the one locality.[3] Actually, the injured party need not be limited to a small local seller; even a seller who markets on a nationwide basis can be considered "injured" by such price discrimination on the part of another nationwide seller.[4]

Another level of competition which may be affected by price discrimination and subjected to a legal test under the Robinson-Patman Act is that between the customers of the seller—the secondary level of competition. If, for example, a manufacturer sells goods to customer A at a lower price than he sells them to customer B in that same market, then customer B is going to be at a market disadvantage in competing with customer A. Customer B would either suffer lower profits in charging the same price for his products as customer A, or would suffer a loss of sales in trying to charge a higher price to cover his higher costs. In any case, customer A would have a better opportunity to increase sales promotion, enhance service, or expand. Thus com-

[3] *Moore v. Mead's Fine Bread Co.,* 348 U.S. 115 (1954).
[4] *H. J. Heinz Co. v. Beech-Nut Life Savers, Inc.,* 181 F. Supp. 452 (1960).

syrup producers who charged higher prices to some candy manufacturers than to others put those candy manufacturers who had
to pay the higher prices at a sufficient disadvantage for the courts
to find a substantial lessening of competition.[5]

A third level of competition to which the Robinson-Patman
Act can be applied is that involving *customers of the customer*
who has received the benefit of a discriminatory price. If a manufacturer discriminates in price in sales to wholesalers with the
result that the competition among the customers of those wholesalers is affected, then the discrimination can be condemned.
Thus, the Federal Trade Commission has prohibited a manufacturer of rubber heels and soles from granting discriminatory
discounts and rebates between purchasers whose customers were
competing with each other in the resale of the products.[6]

## SUBSTANTIAL LESSENING OF COMPETITION

Just what constitutes the adverse competitive conditions which
must be shown by an enforcement agency or private claimant in
order to demonstrate a prohibited effect? Is injury to a competitor the same thing as injury to competition? Elimination of a
competitor may well weaken the competition by removing one of
the rivals. Yet each competitor's objective is, presumably, to outsell his competitors, and this means increasing sales at the competitor's expense. A loss of sales by one business to another is an
inherent part of the competition of the free enterprise system.
Nevertheless, the diversion of trade from one business to another
has in some cases been considered sufficient evidence of the
illegal effect.[7] Legal doctrine tends, however, to profess the view
that policy should be that of preserving competition and not just
competitors.[8] But the two are not mutually exclusive. Evidence

[5] *Corn Products Refining Co. v. Federal Trade Commission,* 324 U.S. 726
(1945), and *A. E. Staley Mfg. Co. v. Federal Trade Commission,* 324 U.S. 746
(1945).

[6] *Holtite Manufacturing Company and Cat's Paw Rubber Company, Inc.,*
50 F.T.C. 379 (1953).

[7] See, for example, *Page Dairy Co.,* 50 F.T.C. 395 (1953); *Magnesium Co.
of America, Inc.,* 52 F.T.C. 623 (1956).

[8] See, for example, *Purex Corporation, Ltd.,* 51 F.T.C. 100, 113 (1954),
and *Anheuser-Busch, Inc. v. Federal Trade Commission,* 289 F.2d 835, 840
(1961).

of a predatory intent to destroy a competitor can help determine whether the competition itself is being injured. Such an intent might be inferred by sustained below-cost selling. Other factors, undoubtedly, may have to be taken into consideration. The number of competitors in the market and the percentage of the market sold by the accused firm obviously may influence the decision; the more competitors there are in the market and the smaller the percentage of the market being sold by the discriminating seller, the more difficult it would be to infer that the price discrimination was predatory in intent and capable of lessening the competition.

According to the Robinson-Patman Act, the effects of a price discrimination must be such that they *may* lessen the competition *substantially*. Price discriminations are not illegal per se. Discriminations which are negligible or have a remote effect on competition are not prohibited.[9] But the prohibited competitive effects do not have to be actual. This is in accord with the antitrust philosophy of the Clayton Act that the law should catch monopoly in its incipiency before the damage is done. The 1948 Morton Salt decision of the Supreme Court held that all that need be shown was a "reasonable possibility" that competition would be adversely affected.[10] A strong dissent in that decision argued for use of "reasonable probability," pointing out the important difference between them.[11] Since that time various courts have relied on either phrase; but whatever the distinction between them, "the two terms seem to have been used somewhat interchangeably."[12] It is perhaps safe to say that it is the probability, and not just the possibility, of injury to competition that governs in most cases.

Another issue is whether the products involved in the dis-

---

[9] *Whitaker Cable Corp. v. Federal Trade Commission*, 239 F.2d 253, 256 (1956), *cert. denied*, 353 U.S. 938 (1957); *E. Edelmann & Co. v. Federal Trade Commission*, 239 F.2d 152, 155 (1956), *cert. denied*, 355 U.S. 941 (1958).

[10] *Federal Trade Commission v. Morton Salt Co.*, 334 U.S. 37, 50 (1948). This phrase was also used, but in contradictory context, in the 1945 decision of the Supreme Court in *Corn Products Refining Co. v. Federal Trade Commission*, 324 U.S. 726, 738, 742 (1945).

[11] *Federal Trade Commission v. Morton Salt Co.*, 334 U.S. 37, 56 (1948).

[12] *H. J. Heinz Co. v. Beech-Nut Life Savers, Inc.*, 181 F. Supp. 452, 460–461 (1960).

crimination are of "like grade and quality." If they are not, then no competition which can be lessened exists in the first place. The products do not have to be identical. But how different must they be to escape the jurisdiction of the act? In view of marketers' efforts to differentiate products in order to complete a full line of products to meet as many different market demands and elasticities as possible, this is a significant question. This product differentiation may involve shape of the product, minor changes in the physical characteristics of the product, packaging, branding, and so on. It is not possible to predict in advance what the enforcement agency or court's decision will be with respect to this matter of "like grade and quality," for their decisions have not always seemed consistent. But an appeals court's 1958 decision offers a logical guide: Artificial distinctions in the product are not enough to make them unlike, but substantial brand or packaging variations are if they make the products appeal to distinct customer classes or cause them to sell in different price ranges.[13] Commodities may thus be of like grade and quality even though they bear different brand names. Nevertheless, the sale of private-label products at prices lower than those of a manufacturer's nationally advertised products is not necessarily unlawful since the former do not have to bear the burden of those advertising expenses.

### GOOD FAITH MEETING OF COMPETITION

Section 2(*b*) of the amended Clayton Act allows a business firm to charge a lower price to one or more of its customers than it does to all the others if such discrimination in price is done "in good faith to meet an equally low price of a competitor." This is a substantive and not just a procedural defense to a charge of price discrimination.[14] This means that if good faith can be shown, the discrimination is not illegal even if there has been a substantial lessening of competition. The burden of proving good faith, however, falls upon the defense.

One problem to be resolved under the good faith defense

[13] *Atalanta Trading Corp. v. Federal Trade Commission,* 258 F.2d 365 (1958).

[14] *Standard Oil Co. v. Federal Trade Commission,* 340 U.S. 231 (1951).

is that of knowing whether there truly *is* a competitive price which needs to be met. A discriminating seller needs to substantiate the competitive prices and to show the actual availability of such prices by competitor(s) ready and willing to move in and take over the customers at those prices.[15] In addition, the seller must be in actual competition with the other sellers who are making the lower prices available. Thus the Sun Oil Company could not grant discriminatory price concessions to certain franchised dealers to help them meet the lower market prices in a gasoline price war. It was Sun's dealers' competitors, not its own, who were cutting the prices.[16]

The good faith proviso raises the question of whether this defense permits a seller to grant discriminatory prices not only to retain existing customers but also to gain new ones. The Federal Trade Commission has taken the position that the law permits only the retention of old customers, i.e., that the good faith defense permits discrimination as a defensive competitive tactic only.[17] The Seventh Circuit Court of Appeals, however, overruled the Commission on this point in 1962, holding that the law does not distinguish between existing and prospective purchasers and that new customers may be obtained through discriminatory pricing.[18] The Commission held, nevertheless, to its position,[19] arguing that its thinking was upheld by a decision of the Second Circuit Court of Appeals.[20] Legal disagreement on a matter such as this serves to bewilder marketers and provides an illustration of the confusion that can arise from the application of regulation to trade.

Disagreement on the economic interpretation of the good faith proviso of the Robinson-Patman Act stems from different interpretations of the nature of "competition." Those who favor

[15] *Federal Trade Commission v. Standard Oil Co.*, 355 U.S. 396 (1958); *Standard Motor Products, Inc. v. Federal Trade Commission*, 265 F.2d 674 (1959), *cert. denied*, 361 U.S. 826 (1959).

[16] *Federal Trade Commission v. Sun Oil Co.*, 83 Sup. Ct. 358 (1963).

[17] *Sunshine Biscuits, Inc.*, Federal Trade Commission Docket 7708 (1961).

[18] *Sunshine Biscuits, Inc. v. Federal Trade Commission*, 306 F.2d 48 (1962).

[19] Federal Trade Commission statement issued Nov. 23, 1962.

[20] *Standard Motor Products, Inc. v. Federal Trade Commission*, 265 F.2d 674 (1959).

permitting price discrimination to obtain new customers argue that a denial to a firm of the right to meet the lower prices of competitors on a discriminatory basis provides those competitors with immunity from price rivalry and thus from competition.[21] It has been argued, on the other hand, that to permit selective price discriminations (except where there is predatory intent) will discourage that price rivalry represented by a seller's lowering his price to *all* customers.[22]

The seller may meet an *equally* low price of a competitor, but he may not undercut a competitor's price. The spirit of the law can rule over the letter of the law, however. When Arden Farms lowered the price on almost all its ice-cream products in the Los Angeles area to meet the competition, it went technically beyond the limits of "meet[ing] an equally low price" by setting prices lower than competitors'. Yet this conduct was excused by the court, which felt that it was a defensive rather than a predatory measure, designed to meet the "chiselling cuts, special advantages and rebates" being given in that market.[23] On the other hand, for a seller to sell on a discriminatory basis small quantities of a commodity at prices which are commensurate only with the larger quantities on the competitor's quantity discount schedule is not considered good faith; it is but an attempt to stretch the letter of the law and amounts to undercutting the price.[24]

The quality or consumer acceptance of a commodity has some bearing on the application of the good faith defense. The cut in price of a so-called "premium" product, which is heavily advertised nationally, to the same level as the price of an off-brand or only locally advertised product might represent in effect a cut in price below that of the competitors. The regular grade

[21] See *Sunshine Biscuits, Inc. v. Federal Trade Commission*, 306 F.2d 48 (1962), and dissenting opinion of Commissioner Elman in *Sunshine Biscuits, Inc.*, Federal Trade Commission Docket 7708 (1961).

[22] See comments of Alfred E. Kahn in *Report of the Attorney General's National Committee to Study the Antitrust Laws*, 1955, pp. 185–186.

[23] *Balian Ice Cream Co., Inc. v. Arden Farms Co.*, 231 F.2d 356, 366 (1955), cert. denied, 350 U.S. 991 (1956).

[24] *Federal Trade Commission v. Standard Brands, Inc.*, 187 F.2d 510 (1951).

of gasoline of a major brand frequently sells at 2 cents above private brands of gasoline under normal competitive conditions; for the major brand seller to meet the same price of the private brand seller can be considered "beating," not "meeting," competition.[25] Also, a district court has said that whether a cut in price of baby foods in glass jars to the same price as baby foods in tins represented undercutting of price rested on whether the public considered the glass-contained product a "premium" product and that that in turn rested on whether the public was generally willing to pay a higher price for the glass-contained product.[26]

Good faith in this context of the "premium" product cannot always be judged by hard-and-fast rules. For example, whereas traditionally the price spread between major and nonmajor brands of gasoline is at least 2 cents per gallon, Sun Oil Company in one instance had selectively reduced price to within 1 cent of the nonmajor brands. The court exonerated Sun from a charge of price discrimination by the Federal Trade Commission, holding that gasoline prices were too volatile and erratic not to admit good faith on Sun's part.[27] Then, again, the Federal Trade Commission issued an order against Anheuser-Busch for selling its Budweiser beer in the St. Louis market at the same prices as the local beers while holding the price of its premium beer up in other regions.[28] But this order was eventually set aside on the grounds that no predatory abuse of power had been involved in Anheuser-Busch's experimental price cut when its overall position was declining.[29]

### MEETING A COMPETITOR'S LAWFUL PRICE

The Robinson-Patman Act makes no mention of a requirement that prices being met in selective discriminations must be lawful

---

[25] *American Oil Co.*, Federal Trade Commission Docket 8183 (1962).

[26] *Gerber Products Co. v. Beech-Nut Life Savers, Inc.*, 160 F. Supp. 916, 921–922 (1958). The issue of whether the public was willing to pay a higher price for the glass-contained product was never resolved in this case.

[27] *Sun Oil Co. v. Federal Trade Commission*, 294 F.2d 465 (1961).

[28] *Anheuser-Busch, Inc.*, 54 F.T.C. 277 (1957).

[29] *Anheuser-Busch, Inc. v. Federal Trade Commission*, 289 F.2d 835 (1961).

prices. Yet the Supreme Court has, in interpreting that act, added the word "lawful" to Section 2(*b*).[30]

Collusive pricing as represented by systematic basing-point pricing provides the clearest illustration of the unlawful price which, when met, cannot qualify under the good faith defense. Under basing-point pricing, each seller knows what the delivered price quoted to any given customer by all sellers will be. The price quoted will be the lowest sum of a base price plus rail freight from that base. Knowing this formula, sellers will absorb freight where necessary to "meet the competition." Since the formula is understood and used by all the sellers party to the arrangement, the price to the customer is not really a competitive price at all; it is, rather, a collusive price. Also, where under the system a nonbase mill includes "phantom freight" charges which were never actually incurred as part of its price to a customer, this cannot, obviously, be considered to be in good faith. To say that this seller is "meeting the competition" is obvious sophistry.[31]

Not all cases are as clear-cut with respect to whether the price being met is a lawful or an unlawful price. In the Standard Oil (Indiana) case the Federal Trade Commission was convinced that the continuation of Standard's discriminatory prices to three jobbers for several years was clear evidence that Standard's pricing was too systematic to be justifiable under good faith.[32] The Supreme Court, however, held that this was a case of continuous recurrence of competitors' price offers in a cutthroat market and that this represented sporadic rather than systematic pricing.[33]

In the Tri-Valley Packing Association order of the Federal Trade Commission, the Commission denied the good faith defense on the grounds that the defense had not indicated whether the prices being met could be cost-justified or otherwise excused under any of the exceptions to the prohibitions of Section 2(*a*) of the Robinson-Patman Act or whether the respondent had reason

---

[30] *Standard Oil Co. v. Federal Trade Commission,* 340 U.S. 231, 238 (1951).

[31] See *A. E. Staley Mfg. Co. v. Federal Trade Commission,* 324 U.S. 746 (1945).

[32] 49 F.T.C. 923 (1953).

[33] 355 U.S. 396 (1958).

to believe that they could be justified.[34] In the American Oil
Company order of the Commission that company was denied
the right to meet a Shell Oil dealer's price because the price of
the Shell gasoline was held to be illegal since it equaled, and
thus undercut, the price of a private brand gasoline.[35] A seller
does not have to *prove* that the price he is meeting is lawful.[36]
But in these last two cases, the Commission assumed that the
respondent, in order to show good faith, must make some study
of the business of the rival whose price is being met in order to
determine whether that price is a lawful price. Such a requirement either limits the extent to which good faith can be utilized
as a defense or is an invitation to a business to find out more
about the rival's affairs than the spirit of the antitrust laws might
approve of.

## QUANTITY DISCOUNTS

Quantity discount schedules or even the granting of quantity
discounts which result from individual instances of bargaining
have a rightful economic place in the sale of commodities when
they are based on cost savings. Such savings are readily apparent
in handling and delivering goods in large volume as compared
with handling and delivering them in small quantities. Most
large business firms show cognizance of this fact in their price
schedules, which provide discounts graduated in accordance with
the size of the purchase. The Robinson-Patman Act makes no
objection to such quantity discount schedules as long as the price
differentials "make only due allowance for differences in the cost
of manufacture, sale, or delivery resulting from the differing
methods or quantities in which such commodities are to such
purchasers sold or delivered." As long as discounts are based on
cost savings, the seller is not violating the law even if competition is substantially lessened or injured. The law, relying on the
assumption that lower selling prices mean lower prices to the
consumer, places the welfare of the consumer above that of the
small buyers who are put at a disadvantage by having to pay

[34] Federal Trade Commission Dockets 7225, 7496 (1962).
[35] Federal Trade Commission Docket 8183 (1962).
[36] *Standard Oil Company v. Brown*, 238 F.2d 54, 58 (1956).

higher prices than their bigger rivals who can demonstrate superior economic efficiency.

The cost proviso of the Robinson-Patman Act permits those price differentials which result from the differing *methods* or *quantities* in which such commodities are sold or delivered. Although the word "manufacture" appears in the proviso, it is relevant only when it affects these differing methods or quantities. The principal drawback of this provision of the act is the difficulty of demonstrating or proving the cost saving. First, the burden of proving it falls upon the seller.[37] Second, this burden generally requires a complete cost study, and conjectural estimates are usually considered inadequate. Third, and most important from the accountant's viewpoint, is the matter of defining the applicable "cost."

What costs are to be allowed to be included in a cost-justification analysis? Are the marketing or distribution costs alone to be considered? Which of the overhead costs are applicable? Are those *buyer's* costs which are saved applicable? Further, how are costs to be allocated among joint products and among classes of customers? These questions are all pertinent because no clear-cut set of rules has evolved by which the sellers of goods can be guided in their preparation of a cost defense. It is clear that marginal or incremental costs alone are not to govern. The Commission's own Advisory Committee on Cost Justification reported to it in 1956 that, in view of the many factors involved and because of the element of opinion and approximation in cost analyses, no specific set of accounting rules should be drawn up. Indeed, price itself may be a factor helping to determine unit costs through its effect on production volume and efficiency. At any rate, largely because of these several difficulties, the record shows that few firms have been able, in litigation, to justify price differences on the basis of cost. And those which have not attempted it have undoubtedly been scared away by the high cost and uncertainty of the effort. If any lesson can be learned from this pessimistic record, it is that the marketer responsible for pricing should work closely with the accountant.

---

[37] *Federal Trade Commission v. Morton Salt Co.*, 334 U.S. 37 (1948).

## QUANTITY LIMITS

The concession of the cost proviso to economies of scale and the consumer interest is partially withdrawn in the provision immediately following in the act which permits the Federal Trade Commission, after due investigation and hearing, to fix and establish quantity limits for particular commodities or classes of commodities where the Federal Trade Commission "finds that available purchasers in greater quantities are so few as to render differentials on account thereof unjustly discriminatory or promotive of monopoly in any line of commerce." Beyond these limits no further discounts could be granted. The Commission, in other words, is authorized to enforce discriminatory prices *against* large buyers.

The Commission first exercised this authority in 1952, establishing a quantity limit of 20,000 pounds (one carload) to the size of single purchases of automobile rubber tires and tubes for delivery at one time.[38] The intention of the Commission was to limit the price advantage that large buyers such as Sears Roebuck were enjoying over the smaller dealer-distributors. Some twenty tire manufacturers or sellers successfully challenged this rule in the courts.[39] The court decisions were based on what were basically technical matters. A principal objection by the courts was that the Commission had not made a proper finding of the fewness of sellers who could afford to buy in quantities larger than the quantity limit which had been set. The Commission had, instead, concentrated on establishing a limit at that quantity which would permit many buyers to obtain the advantage of the maximum discount. It emphasized that there were only 63 buyers who purchased $600,000 or more each year, and 888 buyers who bought more than $100,000 per year. It set the quantity limit, however, at 20,000 pounds purchased at any one time, an entirely different measure. The Commission has not, since its defeat in this case, established another rule, either for that or any other industry. We therefore have no clue to how many sellers constitute the "so few" required by the law.

[38] Federal Trade Commission Quantity Limit Rule 203-1, Jan. 4, 1952.
[39] *B. F. Goodrich Co. v. Federal Trade Commission et al.*, 134 F. Supp. 39 (1955), *affirmed*, 242 F.2d 31 (1957).

## FUNCTIONAL DISCOUNTS

A functional or trade discount is a discount granted to a buyer on the basis of his market status classification, such as that of warehouse distributor, wholesaler, jobber, educational institution, fleet operator, or retailer. The Robinson-Patman Act makes no reference to functional discounts. It might be thought that these buyers performing different functions would not be in competition with each other and therefore would have no effect on the competition. But in actuality injury to competition can occur in two principal areas as the result of the granting of functional discounts.

The first area of competitive inequality arising from the giving of functional discounts is that in which different functional categories may be represented by buyers who, at least in part of their trade, are in competition with each other. Oil jobbers, for example, sometimes also sell at retail, and they may use their functional discount received as jobbers to advantage in the competition with retailers. Or a wholesaler of roofing materials may also be engaged in the business of installing roofing in competition with roofers. Second, the practice of dual distribution may create competitive inequalities. An oil refiner, for example, may sell gasoline at a tank-car price to a jobber who in turn sells at a tank-wagon price to retailers while other retailers are buying directly from the refiner at the refiner's tank-wagon price. If the wholesaler's and the refiner's tank-wagon prices are not the same, then the competitive opportunities between the two groups of retailers will not be equal. Whenever a manufacturer operates on the basis of a system of dual distribution, there is the possibility that the competition "with customers of either of them" will be affected in this manner.

The second possible area of competitive inequality arises from the functional classification of a buyer. This classification and any accompanying functional discount is influenced partly by the individual bargaining. Where the functional status of a buyer is not clear-cut and where the buyer's operations as a seller cut across more than one market level, the buyer can perhaps bargain for that status which will yield the largest discount. In other words, a buyer may be receiving discounts in the name of a seller's customer classification when he is not fully functionally eligible for it. Also, it is possible that a seller may grant these discounts as a tool in predatory competition with other sellers. The fact that the buying and selling functions of sellers under modern, changing marketing conditions are somewhat scrambled contributes to the complexity of making a proper analysis of the legitimacy of a trade discount.

If the statute makes no reference to functional discounts, how can the law exert control over the inequitable discriminations that may result from them? It relies on the provision of the Robinson-Patman Act which condemns a substantial lessening of or injury to the competition. Where competition is adversely affected by trade discounts, these discounts can be condemned. The seller's only defenses lie in the cost savings or the good faith meeting of competition provisos. Presumably, where certain marketing functions are truly being performed, there will be cost savings to the seller involved, and the Federal Trade Commission should try to analyze the function in these terms. But functional discounts per se carry no legal weight.

Attempted enforcement of the price discrimination law can lead to awkward results where functional discounts are involved. In the Standard Oil (Indiana) case the Federal Trade Commission found that discounts to jobbers were being passed on in lower tank-wagon prices to retailers with the result that price competition between these retailers and Standard's own retail customers was becoming severe. The Commission held that the diversion of business to the jobbers' retailers from Standard's retailers represented an injury to competition. To avoid this injury the Commission ordered Standard to cease the price difference if the jobbers were selling to their retailers at lower prices than Standard was selling to its own retailers. In effect, the Commission order required Standard either to cease its dual distribution selling or to police resale price maintenance.[40] The latter course of action amounts to price control which, except for the fair trade laws, is prohibited under the antitrust laws. The choice never had to be made by Standard, however, because the case

[40] 41 F.T.C. 263, 284–285 (1945); 43 F.T.C. 56, 58 (1946); 49 F.T.C. 923, 956 (1953) ; 173 F.2d 210, 217 (1949) .

eventually hinged on the good faith meeting of competition and was resolved in favor of Standard Oil.[41] Where the problem of discriminatory pricing derives from the split function of the buyer who is engaged in both wholesaling and retailing, an easy solution, to which the Federal Trade Commission has resorted, lies in limiting the discount to that part of the buyer's sales which are made at wholesale.[42] It is a solution, however, based on character of selling rather than on cost of service and efficiency.

## BROKERAGE DISCOUNTS

A broker is a person or firm paid a fee or commission for acting as an agent in consummating sales. He is found principally in the food industry. The function of the broker is to bring together buyers and sellers. As an agent for a seller, the broker finds market outlets for the seller's goods. As an agent for a buyer, the broker searches out and finds sources of supply. Brokerage is the pecuniary reward received by the broker from the buyer or seller for the rendering of such services. In the case of the food broker, who acts as the seller's agent, the commission or fee is generally treated by the seller in his accounts as a selling expense. If the buyer were to be permitted to perform the brokerage function himself, he would deduct an amount from the seller's price to compensate for the performance of that function. This is a brokerage discount.

Brokerage discounts or allowances are not permitted by Section 2(c) of the Robinson-Patman Act where either the buyer or the seller is in any way, directly or indirectly, affiliated with the intermediary providing the brokerage service. This is a flat prohibition.[43] It is illegal per se for a seller to pay any commission or broker's fee, "or any allowance or discount in lieu thereof," to a buyer.

The purpose of this brokerage provision of the law was to

[41] 355 U.S. 396 (1958).

[42] See, for example, *American Oil Company,* 29 F.T.C. 857 (1939); and *Sherwin-Williams Company,* 36 F.T.C. 25 (1943).

[43] *Great Atlantic & Pacific Tea Co. v. Federal Trade Commission,* 106 F.2d 667, 674 (1939); *Federal Trade Commission v. Simplicity Pattern Co., Inc.,* 360 U.S. 55, 65 (1959).

prevent the use by large buyers of brokerage fees, often through dummy brokers, as a mask to cover up discriminatory price reductions secured in their favor which might run afoul of the Clayton Act. Large firms, such as A & P, buying in large quantities and possessing more market contacts and knowledge than small firms, were able to bypass independent brokerage firms and secure the brokerage equivalent for themselves. For this reason Section 2(*c*) prohibits brokerage "or any allowance or discount in lieu thereof" to any party other than a truly independent broker. Judicial interpretation of the legislative intent has caused the phrase within Section 2(*c*) "except for services rendered" to be a dead letter, on the assumption that only a broker could perform services for which "brokerage" might be paid.[44] Intended to provide protection against the large buyer for the small businessman, Section 2(*c*) also provides a more secure market for the independent brokers.

The absolute prohibition against brokerage or an allowance in lieu thereof being paid to the buyer who performs the brokerage function himself represents an economic discrimination against that buyer. His market efforts or efficiency are being denied reimbursement or reward. He must pay the same price as those buyers who are being served by independent brokers.

The brokerage provision, which both curbs the buying power of large firms and denies them rewards for economic efficiency, has also had an adverse impact upon small buyers. Efforts of small grocers to form joint organizations in order to serve the brokerage function, such as purchasing cooperatives or corporations whose stock is held by otherwise independent grocers, have been thwarted; for distribution of the price reductions received by such joint buying organizations to their members in the form of patronage dividends, corporate dividends, or advertising allowances has been held to be receipt of illegal brokerage.[45] Thus a provision of the law which was essentially designed to

[44] *Great Atlantic & Pacific Tea Co. v. Federal Trade Commission,* 106 F.2d 667, 674–675 (1939), *cert. denied,* 308 U.S. 625 (1940); *Webb-Crawford Co. v. Federal Trade Commission,* 109 F.2d 268, 270 (1940).

[45] See, for example, *Independent Grocers Alliance Distributing Co. v. Federal Trade Commission,* 203 F.2d 941 (1953); and *Modern Marketing Service, Inc. v. Federal Trade Commission,* 149 F.2d 970 (1945).

protect small businessmen from the superior bargaining power of the large buyer now prevents them from seeking price concessions through "brokerage" payments.

The 1960 Henry Broch decision of the Supreme Court bears seeds of possible change in these rigidities imposed by the brokerage provision of the Robinson-Patman Act.[46] In this case a seller's broker agreed with the seller, and without the knowledge of the buyer, to reduce his commission from 5 to 3 per cent, so that the price to the buyer might be reduced. The price to buyers and the brokerage rate remained unchanged on all other sales. The court held that this reduction of the brokerage fee in order to help make possible the reduced price to the buyer by the seller was just as much a violation of Section 2(c) as when the seller absorbs the full reduction in price alone. The seller's broker is clearly "any person" as per the words of Section 2(c). The buyer is only concerned with getting a price concession; he does not care whether it comes from the seller, the seller's broker, or both. The court rejected the argument that the seller is free to pass on to the buyer any differential represented by reduced brokerage fees; once an action is condemned under Section 2(c), it cannot be justified under Section 2(a). "Section 2(c) . . . is independent of §2(a)." Congress enacted Section 2(c), said the court, because Section 2(a) was not considered adequate to deal with abuses of the brokerage function. Thus, the decision in the Broch case did not change essentially the state of the law of Section 2(c). It simply applied it to the seller's broker as well as to the seller, even though the allowances were made indirectly through the seller.

But comments of the majority in the Broch decision have raised speculation as to the direction of future decisions. The court noted that there was no evidence that the buyer had rendered any services to the seller or to the seller's broker or that anything in the buyer's method of dealing justified its getting a price concession through a reduced brokerage charge. "We would have quite a different case if there were such evidence and we need not explore the applicability of §2(c) to such circum-

---

[46] *Federal Trade Commission v. Henry Broch & Co.*, 363 U.S. 166 (1960). This was a 5 to 4 decision.

stances."[47] And, further: "This is not to say that every reduction in price, coupled with a reduction in brokerage, automatically compels the conclusion that an allowance 'in lieu' of brokerage has been granted."[48] In other words, it might well be that it could be shown that there were true cost savings attributable to the buyer and that the resulting discriminatory price would be legal. If this were so, as dissenting opinion in the case believed it should be, then the cost-justification provision of Section 2(*a*) would become operative.

It is possible, then, that a broad interpretation of the Broch decision will revitalize the "except for services rendered" of Section 2(*c*). If true cost savings are permitted to be justified, i.e., if all price differences are not to be condemned out of hand as being "allowances in lieu of brokerage," then greater flexibility of prices would be provided for. Cooperative buying groups of small businessmen might well be able to demonstrate services rendered and justify their existence, and a freer hand would be provided to seek out optimum marketing methods.

## PROMOTIONAL ALLOWANCES AND SERVICES

Two market practices which are amenable to use as devices for discrimination among business customers are (1) the granting of money allowances to buyers in return for services or facilities furnished by the buyer toward the promotion and resale of the supplier's goods and (2) the granting of services or facilities to the buyer toward the promotion and resale of the supplier's goods. These cooperative promotional arrangements designed to aid the resale of products will be discriminatory if they are not made available to all buyers on a relative but similar basis. Obviously these allowances cannot be made available to all customers on the same absolute basis; buyers differ in terms of size of both physical establishment and volume of sales, the latter particularly with respect to a given supplier's goods. The law insists that the sellers make these allowances and services available to all purchasers "on proportionally equal terms." These are the provisions of Sections 2(*d*) and 2(*e*), respectively, of the Rob-

---

[47] *Ibid.*, p. 173.
[48] *Ibid.*, p. 175.

inson-Patman Act. They are designed to ensure equitable treatment of all buyers and to prevent such allowances or services being used as a subterfuge for lower prices to favored customers. They are absolute provisions of law. No injury to competition need be shown, and the cost justification of Section 2(*a*) cannot be used as a defense.[49] However, the good faith meeting of competition defense is available to charges of not making promotional allowances[50] or services[51] proportionally available.

Advertising allowances account for the largest share of the promotional allowances which are paid by suppliers to customers. Purchasers may be paid for placing advertisements featuring the supplier's particular products in local newspapers, on television, or on radio stations. Promotional monies may also be used to pay for such things as poster displays and circulars, special display racks, and demonstrators. Most of this promotion money goes to the big department-store retailers.

Whereas the large retailer may receive a sizable allowance from his supplier for advertising purposes, the small retailer more often has to pay for his own. Discriminatory payments for advertising and promotional allowances have been particularly evident by wearing-apparel manufacturers and distributors, and the Federal Trade Commission succeeded in getting almost two hundred such sellers to sign consent decrees to cease such practices in 1963.

Services or facilities furnished by suppliers to customers may be advertising, promotion materials such as display cabinets and racks, giveaway premiums and merchandise, and demonstrators. The problem is to avoid discrimination. A clothes stylist may be assigned to a certain department store by a manufacturer of branded female clothing. This provides a competitive advantage to that particular retail outlet. Yet it is also economically not feasible for the manufacturer to provide such services to all outlets.

[49] *Federal Trade Commission v. Simplicity Pattern Co., Inc.*, 360 U.S. 55 (1959).

[50] *Exquisite Form Brassiere, Inc. v. Federal Trade Commission*, 301 F.2d 499 (1961).

[51] *Federal Trade Commission v. Simplicity Pattern Co., Inc.*, 360 U.S. 55 (1959).

The intricacies and technicalities of applying the law to trade are well illustrated by examining the conditions which must be considered before a marketer can grant promotional allowances or furnish services or facilities and still know that he is on the right side of the law. First, before a charge of such forms of discrimination can be made successfully, interstate commerce must be shown to be involved.[52] This is not difficult, for intrastate sales can easily be considered to have an effect on, and thus be considered to be in, interstate commerce.[53]

Second, the customers among whom the discriminatory treatment has been charged as having taken place must be in competition with each other.[54] This question involves several elements. The geographical location of the buyers obviously is a factor for consideration. A retail store in Arizona is not in competition with one in Maine. But two mail-order houses, no matter where located, are in competition. The time of the sales is also a factor. If advertising allowances are granted one month, they do not have to be granted to another seller five months later. Otherwise the initial allowance granted would determine all future such grants.[55] The products to which allowances pertain must be of like grade and quality. A seller does not have to grant promotion allowances on his whole line of products; he can promote only one if he so desires.[56] Another related question involves the functional classification of customers. Ordinarily the "customer" or "purchaser" referred to in the law is the one who buys directly from the seller or his agent or broker.[57] But are wholesalers in

[52] Section 2(e) contains no "in commerce" expression, but this has been ruled a mere inadvertence. *Elizabeth Arden Sales Corp. v. Gus Blass Co.*, 150 F.2d 988 (1945).

[53] See *Corn Products Refining Co. v. Federal Trade Commission*, 324 U.S. 726 (1945).

[54] Section 2(e) lacks the phrase "customers competing in the distribution of such products or commodities" which appears in Section 2(d), but the Supreme Court made a finding of competition in a Section 2(e) case. *Federal Trade Commission v. Simplicity Pattern Co., Inc.*, 360 U.S. 55 (1959). The Federal Trade Commission points out in its Guides for Allowances and Services that allowances and services need only be provided to competing customers.

[55] *Atalanta Trading Corp. v. Federal Trade Commission*, 258 F.2d 365 (1958).

[56] *Ibid.*

[57] Federal Trade Commission Guides for Allowances and Services.

competition with retailers? A district court has decided that the promotion-allowances provision was violated when a manufacturer gave a retailer an allowance without giving one to a wholesaler whose customers competed with that retailer.[58] On the other hand, a retailer who purchased from a manufacturer's wholly owned subsidiary and did not receive promotional allowances as favorable as those of retailers buying direct from that manufacturer was unable to prove a violation of Section 2(*d*) because it had not been shown that the discriminations were made by the same seller.[59]

Third, a seller must be aware that indirect, as well as direct, payments for the benefit of a customer are likely to come in conflict with the law. Such an illegal arrangement is represented by payments by the Swanee Paper Corporation for space available on a Times Square "spectacular sign" utilized by the Grand Union grocery chain. Grand Union received no allowances from Swanee, but was still receiving the benefit.[60]

A fourth consideration is to understand and comply with the requirement of "on proportionally equal terms." Proportional to what? The law does not say. The Federal Trade Commission's guide on this matter states that generally this requirement can best be met by basing the payments made or the services furnished on the dollar volume or on the quantity of goods purchased during a specified time. Advertising allowances for advertisements in newspapers present no peculiar problems. For example, a manufacturer can offer to pay a certain percentage of the cost of the advertising up to an amount equal to, say, 5 per cent of the dollar volume of purchases. The furnishing of demonstrators to large department stores poses more of a problem, for such facilities may not also be adaptable to use by small retail outlets. To meet this problem, the manufacturer must make available usable alternatives. The alternative plans must be reasonably practical for and made available to all groups of customers, and due notice of this availability must be given. A

[58] *Krug v. International Telephone & Telegraph Corp.*, 142 F. Supp. 230 (1956).

[59] *Baim & Blank, Inc. v. Philco Corp.*, 148 F. Supp. 541 (1957).

[60] *Swanee Paper Corporation v. Federal Trade Commission*, 291 F.2d 833 (1961).

money advertising allowance or displays might satisfy this requirement. If monies are granted for such purposes, the seller must ensure that they are used for such purposes. Indeed, a customer may become liable under Section 2(f) if such monies are not used for their designated purpose.[61]

## PRICE DISCRIMINATION AND BUYER'S LIABILITY

Section 2(f) of the Robinson-Patman Act makes it unlawful for a buyer "knowingly to induce or receive a discrimination in price which is prohibited by this section." This provision of the act is the only one that emphasizes the basic reason for the passage of the law, namely, the tremendous bargaining power residing in the hands of large, powerful buyers by which they can demand discounts not received by smaller buyers. In 1956, for example, the Union News Company, which operated (in 1958) some 930 newsstands and held a position of "near-dominance" in the retail newsstand field, was found to be demanding rebates representing a steep increase over promotional allowances customarily paid. The circulation manager of *Modern Photography* magazine, in response to a demand for a 10 per cent sales rebate on the retail price of the magazine, agreed reluctantly to the rebate, writing to Union News: "I assume that if this new rate is unacceptable to us, our magazine would not be distributed on your outlets. In view of this situation we have no recourse but to say yes."[62]

Whereas the real offender has been the big buyer, the principal attack of the act is against the seller. Perhaps this is inevitable, for how, it may be asked, can a buyer know or even be expected to know whether his bargaining is yielding him larger discounts, perhaps in the form of rebates, than other buyers are receiving? Or how, even if he does know this, can he know whether or not these price differences are justified by cost differences for the seller or whether the discrimination will be sufficiently injurious to competition?

Experience under this section of the act is limited. The

[61] Federal Trade Commission Guides for Allowances and Services.
[62] *American News Co. and The Union News Co. v. Federal Trade Commission*, 300 F.2d 104, 107, 110 (1962).

Federal Trade Commission has initiated few proceedings with respect to coercive bargaining by buyers. But the Supreme Court has spoken on the issue and in its decision has provided certain guidelines for those who either have to enforce the act or have to conduct their businesses within the framework of the act.[63] In turn, these guidelines will have to be delineated more clearly through the interpretive process of litigation.

To violate the buyer's liability section of the act, a buyer must be reasonably aware of or have knowledge of the illegality of the lower price he has received. But this does not mean that the buyer must know, for example, the seller's cost data; it is up to the Commission to produce such data. Rather, a reasonable awareness on the part of the buyer is required, and this hinges on what that buyer should be expected to know concerning market conditions. If the buyer is purchasing in the same quantities and under similar conditions of delivery as some other buyers but is receiving a substantial price difference, then he should know that he is likely violating the law. If the buyer purchases in different quantities or is served in a different manner from other buyers by the seller, he should be alert to what might be the legitimate cost differences. The magnitude of the discrepancy between the price differential and the cost differential should provide a buyer with some clue about his liability under the act. As for the seller's good faith, the buyer presumably is close enough to that situation to know the facts. In short, the complaining party must show not only the illegality of the discrimination from the seller's point of view, but also that the buyer had reason to know of that illegality.

Buyer's liability under Section 2(*f*) is limited to "a discrimination in price which is prohibited by this section." Does this discrimination in price include the indirect price discriminations implicit in the promotional concessions declared unlawful in Sections 2(*d*) and 2(*e*)? The Federal Trade Commission has successfully issued orders against buyers with respect to promotional receipts, but it has done so by using Section 5 of the Fed-

[63] *Automatic Canteen Co. of America v. Federal Trade Commission,* 346 U.S. 61 (1953).

eral Trade Commission Act, which forbids "unfair methods of competition."[64] The Commission's hesitancy in using Section 2(*f*) of the Robinson-Patman Act for that purpose was suggested as unnecessary, however, by the court, which noted that the omission of buyers from coverage with respect to promotional allowances was an inadvertence not consistent with the original legislative intent of the act.

## ADDENDUM

The many provisos and conditions set forth in the Robinson-Patman Act are not conducive to making its application an easy matter. In the words of Justice Jackson:

> To determine which of its overlapping and conflicting policies shall govern a particular case involves inquiry into grades and qualities of goods, discriminations and their economic effects on interstate commerce, competition between customers, the economic effect of price differentials to lessen competition or tend to create a monopoly, allowance for differences in cost of manufacturing, sale or delivery and good faith in meeting of the price, services or facilities of competitors.[65]

And, he added, the act is "complicated and vague in itself."[66]

The confusion which can easily arise when a business tries to comply with the terms of the Robinson-Patman Act has aroused much adverse comment, not only from professional critics, but also from business and its attorneys. For the larger business firms especially, the act places some constraint upon flexibility in pricing, to a degree which may perhaps be antithetical to the philosophy of antitrust. Before a marketer risks granting price differences, he will be well advised to consult his attorney, if not an accountant as well. Small business, too, has some reason to be disenchanted with the act, for it has prevented maneuvers of small businesses in the marketplace. In addition, a

[64] *The Grand Union Co. v. Federal Trade Commission,* 300 F.2d 92 (1962), and *American News Co. and The Union News Co. v. Federal Trade Commission,* 300 F.2d 104 (1962).

[65] *Federal Trade Commission v. Ruberoid Co.,* 343 U.S. 470, 483–484 (1952).

[66] *Ibid.*

considerable part of the proceedings brought and orders issued under the act have been against relatively small business firms.[67]

## SUGGESTIONS FOR FURTHER READING

The most complete works on the Robinson-Patman Act are Corwin D. Edwards, *The Price Discrimination Law,* The Brookings Institution, Washington, D.C., 1959 (on the economic impact); and Frederick M. Rowe, *Price Discrimination under the Robinson-Patman Act,* Oppenheim Trade Regulation Series, Little, Brown and Company, Boston, 1962 (on the legal principles). A short summary of the first twenty years' experience under the Robinson-Patman Act is available in Corwin D. Edwards, "Twenty Years of the Robinson-Patman Act," *Journal of Business,* July, 1956.

A case-by-case analysis of cost defenses attempted under the Robinson-Patman Act is presented in Herbert F. Taggart, *Cost Justification,* Bureau of Business Research, University of Michigan, Ann Arbor, Mich., 1959. Discussion of injury to competition under Robinson-Patman Act litigation can be found in Robert C. Brooks, Jr., "Businessmen's Concepts of 'Injury to Competition'," *California Management Review,* Summer, 1961; Note on "Competitive Injury under the Robinson-Patman Act," *Harvard Law Review,* June, 1961; and Charles F. Phillips, Jr., and George R. Hall, "Good Faith, Discrimination and Market Organization," *Southern Economic Journal,* October, 1963.

For differing views on the position of the big buyer, see J. B. Dirlam and A. E. Kahn, "Antitrust Law and the Big Buyer: Another Look at the A & P Case," *Journal of Political Economy,* April, 1952; and M. A. Adelman, "The A & P Case: A Study in Applied Economic Theory," *Quarterly Journal of Economics,* May, 1949. A book-length study of A & P's experience with the law is Adelman's *A & P: A Study in Price-Cost Behavior and Public Policy,* Harvard University Press, Cambridge, Mass., 1959.

For comment on the Federal Trade Commission's establishment of quantity limits in the rubber tire industry, see Warren W. Leigh, "The Quantity Limit Rule and the Rubber Tire Industry," *Journal of Marketing,* October, 1952; and John S. McGee, "The Decline and Fall of Quantity Discounts: The Quantity Limit Rule in Rubber Tires and Tubes," *Journal of Business,* July, 1954.

---

[67] See Corwin D. Edwards, "Twenty Years of the Robinson-Patman Act," *Journal of Business,* July, 1956, pp. 153–154; and Frederick M. Rowe, *Price Discrimination under the Robinson-Patman Act,* Little, Brown and Company, Boston, 1962, pp. 536–543.

# 4

# *CONTROLLING*
# *DISTRIBUTION*

Agreements among competitors to control the distribution process by dividing business among themselves are clearly attempts to restrict competition and are per se violations of the Sherman Act. Division of markets among presumably independent competitors by allocating territories in which to sell or buy, the allocation of customers, agreed-upon rotation of bids or orders, agreement on the proportion of total sales or purchases to be made by each firm, and the allocation of the particular products to be produced and sold by each firm are all unreasonable restraints of trade in themselves. Would-be competitors, under such agreements, are acting as one (monopoly) rather than as business rivals. The legal thinking which explains the illegality of such agreements is essentially the same as that which makes price-fixing illegal per se (which we examined in Chapter 2).

In this chapter we shall examine the application of the Federal law to the several types of acquisitions and contractual arrangements which corporate manufacturers or distributors might wish to complete in an effort to give them some degree of control over the flow of goods toward the ultimate consumer. A firm may acquire the assets or capital stock of a competitor or customer or may acquire a new line of products by purchase. A buyer and a seller may form a joint venture. Mutual buyer-seller relationships in the marketplace may be used to facilitate market transactions. Close business ties can be achieved between a buyer and a seller by various forms of contractual integration.

None of these arrangements is free from the jurisdiction and scrutiny of the antitrust laws. A business firm may not freely purchase assets or capital stock of any other business firm which it pleases (assuming the other party wishes to sell) even though "sound business reasons" may be found for such a purchase. Nor can sellers sign contracts with buyers which tie those buyers to those particular suppliers without running the risk of running afoul of some provision of the antitrust laws. Even buyer-seller reciprocity arrangements may be violative of the law.

At the Federal level, the Sherman Act can be utilized to attack these acquisitions and agreements as unreasonable restraints of trade (Section 1) or as monopolizing or attempts to monopolize (Section 2). And the ubiquitous Section 5 of the Federal Trade Commission Act can condemn them under the very broad category of unfair methods of competition. But the Clayton Act is more specific and thus more directly related to these acquisitions and arrangements. The Antimerger (Celler-Kefauver) Act of 1950, amending Section 7 of the Clayton Act of 1914, prohibits a corporation from acquiring the whole or any part of the stock or assets "of another corporation engaged also in commerce, where in any line of commerce in any section of the country, the effect of such acquisition may be substantially to lessen competition, or tend to create a monopoly." Section 3 of the Clayton Act of 1914 makes it unlawful "to lease or make a sale or contract for sale of goods, wares, merchandise, machinery, supplies, or other commodities" on the condition that the lessee or purchaser shall not use or deal in the goods of competitors "where the effect of such lease, sale, or contract for sale or such condition, agreement, or understanding may be to substantially lessen competition or tend to create a monopoly in any line of commerce." Section 3 applies only to the lease, sale, or contract for sale of a commodity; a contract of agency is not covered by this law.

Some state antitrust laws may also prove to be applicable to such acquisitions and agreements. Louisiana, Mississippi, New Jersey, and Washington have statutory provisions against stock acquisitions where the result may be to lessen competition substantially or tend to create a monopoly. Washington statutes prohibit the acquisition of assets and exclusive dealing arrangements where that same result ensues. A Mississippi law covers the acquisition of assets, but only of competing corporations. Kansas has a statute which provides that a sale shall not be conditional upon the exclusion of the goods of any other person. Wyoming has a statute prohibiting the purchase of one good hinging upon the purchase of another from the same seller. But state antitrust laws specific with respect to acquisitions or exclusive dealing arrangements are few, and we shall not be concerned with them here.

## HORIZONTAL MERGER

For competitors to merge their assets or stock and become part of the same corporate organization or group is illegal only where the effect may be to substantially lessen competition. A double standard is thus being applied under the law. Price-fixing and division of markets among competitors have come to be treated as illegal per se; yet a merger among competitors accomplishes the same result in the marketplace.

What mergers among firms at the same level of competition will be permissible depends upon the tests of illegality developed by the prosecuting agencies of the government and the interpretations by the courts of cases brought before them. The Celler-Kefauver Act of 1950 amended Section 7 of the Clayton Act to include asset as well as stock acquisition and broadened its definition of the market; it is relatively new and its effective extent is still being tested. The objective of the act is to check monopoly in its incipiency. The illegal merger will be the one which will be expected to have significantly adverse economic market effects. To determine this, numerous factors must be considered: the relevant geographic market, the number of sellers in the market, the size and character of the companies involved and their relative market positions, the economies of scale in the industry, and the products being sold and their substitutability. One or more of these or other factors may be important in determining a particular case. Most decisions are based on more than a single test. The view that the enforcing agency or courts may take of the particular facts will be important in the ultimate decision.

From the experience of the early years under the new Section 7, one matter is clear: the enforcing agencies have devoted the lion's share of their limited resources to attacking mergers involving the larger firms. This is to be expected. The anti-merger law does not contain statutory limitations. Each case has to be decided on its own merits. The enforcing agencies have to be selective; they cannot attack every merger because there are too many (over 1,000 per year in the early 1960s). Only 96 cases have been brought by the Federal Trade Commission and the Department of Justice during the first eleven years under the new Section 7. But of these, 59 involved the horizontal merger only, and 24 contained horizontal and vertical aspects.[1]

No rigid rule of thumb can be set down about the vulnerability of a large firm with respect to mergers. Reasons can be found to excuse from complaint or violation a merger involving a large firm. The "failing company" doctrine, in which the acquisition of a company on the verge of failure is not to be condemned under Section 7, can be relied upon.[2] The mergers in 1954 of Studebaker with Packard and of Hudson with Nash (American Motors) were both favorably viewed by the Department of Justice and the Federal Trade Commission, even though all four firms were large in absolute terms, on the grounds that they might have a better chance to survive in the competition with General Motors, Ford, and Chrysler. A district court refused to support the government complaint against the merger of Ling-Temco and Chance-Vought because, in view of the broad range of heterogeneous products the two firms were engaged in selling, the amount of direct competition between them was held to be very small.[3]

Market position can be singled out, however, as an important variable affecting a firm's vulnerability to a Section 7 violation. More than half of the cases have been directed against firms

[1] Betty Bock, *Mergers and Markets*, 2d ed., National Industrial Conference Board, New York, 1962, p. 31.

[2] *Brown Shoe Co. v. United States*, 370 U.S. 294, 331 (1962). This doctrine was enunciated under the old Section 7 in *International Shoe Co. v. Federal Trade Commission*, 280 U.S. 291 (1930).

[3] *United States v. Ling-Temco Electronics, Inc.*, Trade Reg. Rep., par. 70,160 (N.D. Tex., 1961).

which ranked first in their industry. A principal objective of antitrust policy under Section 7 appears to be to arrest the creation of monopolies in their incipiency by preventing further concentration in industry. The first new Section 7 case of the government to be adjudicated by a district court was the proposal of Bethlehem Steel Corporation, number two in the steel industry, to merge with Youngstown Sheet & Tube Company, number six in the industry. The court, rejecting the plan, commented:

> The merger offers an incipient threat of setting into motion a chain reaction of further mergers by the other but less powerful companies in the steel industry. If there is logic to the defendants' contention that their joindure is justified to enable them, in their own language, to offer "challenging competition to United States Steel . . . which exercises dominant influence over competitive conditions in the steel industry . . .," then the remaining large producers in the "Big Twelve" could with equal logic urge that they, too, be permitted to join forces and to concentrate their economic resources in order to give more effective competition to the enhanced "Big Two"; and so we reach a point of more intense concentration in an industry already highly concentrated—indeed we head in the direction of triopoly.[4]

Similarly, in the Brown Shoe case, the first of the new Section 7 cases to come before the Supreme Court, the acquisition of the twelfth largest shoe manufacturer, G. R. Kinney Company, Inc., by the fourth largest, Brown Shoe Company, was denied, even though Brown Shoe accounted for only 4 per cent of the national output of shoes and Kinney about 0.5 per cent:

> Congress was desirous of preventing the formation of further oligopolies with their attendant adverse effects upon local control of industry and upon small business. Where an industry was composed of numerous independent units, Congress appeared anxious to preserve this structure. . . . We cannot fail to recognize Congress' desire to promote competition through the protection of viable, small, locally owned businesses.[5]

The Supreme Court was intent upon preventing the shoe industry, although a "fragmented" rather than an oligopolistic

---

[4] *United States v. Bethlehem Steel*, 168 F. Supp. 576, 618–619 (1958).

[5] *Brown Shoe Co. v. United States*, 370 U.S. 294, 333 (1962). Combined retail outlets in some communities exceeded 20 per cent in several cases. Brown Shoe Company was also a very large firm in absolute terms, being one of the top 300 firms in the country in terms of sales. In addition, the case had vertical as well as horizontal aspects.

industry, from experiencing any further tendency toward concentration.

## ACQUISITION OF PRODUCTS

One means of increasing total sales is to purchase assets which
will enable the firm to add to its line of products. The acquisition might involve a conglomerate merger in which the nature
of the acquired firm or product might seem not to be too closely
related to the firm's preexistent nature. The purpose of the merger might be diversification. But any acquisition is subject to
possible scrutiny by those entrusted with the enforcement of the
antitrust laws. A large firm, especially, must consider the possible
antitrust implications. No general rules, however, can be laid
down about the legality of such an acquisition. As long as Section 7 of the Clayton Act covers acquisitions "in any line of
commerce in any section of the country," any acquisition involving a substantial volume of business may be subjected to the
question of whether it is in violation of the law.

Lever Brothers' 1957 acquisition of the trademark of the
low-sudsing, heavy-duty detergent "all" and the patents relating
to "all" from the Monsanto Chemical Company were challenged
by the Department of Justice as a violation of Section 7. With
the acquisition, Lever Brothers' market share of the heavy-duty
detergent market increased from 16.5 to 21.1 per cent between
1956 and 1960. But the district court ruled that the acquisition
did not violate the law.[6] The relevant market, said the court,
was that of "low-sudsing heavy-duty detergents," that is, a
submarket of "heavy-duty detergents." Lever Brothers had no
such product at the time of the acquisition; Monsanto had
not been an effective competitor in its efforts to sell "all"; and
Lever Brothers was an active competitor which vigorously pro-
moted, advertised, and improved the product. In the eyes of the
court, therefore, the acquisition had aided, rather than impeded,
competition.

Somewhat different, yet allied, circumstances are presented
in a second case. The Federal Trade Commission in 1963 issued

---

[6] *United States v. Lever Brothers Company and Monsanto Chemical
Company,* 216 F. Supp. 887 (1963).

an order against The Procter & Gamble Company which would require that company to divest itself of The Clorox Chemical Company, which it had acquired in 1957 through an exchange of stock, ruling that the acquisition violated Section 7 of the Clayton Act.[7] The order stated that Procter & Gamble, whose principal products were food, toiletries, and paper products, could now use its tremendous marketing and advertising power to promote the sales of Clorox, a household liquid bleach of the formerly independent Clorox Chemical Company. Prior to acquisition Clorox had achieved a leading position (48.8 per cent of the market) in the household liquid-bleach industry. After the acquisition, Clorox was in an even more powerful position, as it was now able to exert a more aggressive marketing policy. And Procter & Gamble was eliminated as a potential competitor of Clorox. Procter & Gamble's power derived from its ability to command consumer acceptance of its products and to acquire and retain valuable shelf space in grocery stores. It would now also be in a position to use Clorox as a tying product, loss-leader, or cross-coupon offering. In more general terms, Procter & Gamble had the power to shift its financial resources and competitive strength from one product or market to another. Entry of new competitors would now be more difficult, and there would be an increasing tendency toward concentration and monopoly in the industry. And, in the opinion of the Commission, the marketing economies of large-scale advertising which served only to entrench large market leaders were not socially beneficial.

A complaint involving a conglomerate merger was issued by the Federal Trade Commission in 1963 against General Foods Corporation.[8] General Foods had acquired in 1957 the S.O.S. Company, the dominant producer of household steel wool. The acquisition of this product put General Foods into a new line of business. Concentration in the household steel-wool industry was already high at the time of the acquisition. S.O.S. had 51 per cent of the national market, the second largest producer had 47.6 per cent of that market, and the remaining percentage was divided among only three other producers. Between the time of

---

[7] *The Procter & Gamble Co.*, Federal Trade Commission Docket 6901.
[8] *General Foods Corp.*, Federal Trade Commission Docket 8600.

the acquisition in 1957 and the end of 1961, S.O.S. increased its market share to 57 per cent. The complaint charged that the acquisition might substantially lessen competition or tend to create a monopoly because of any one or all of the following factors: General Foods' dominant market position, financial resources, advertising ability and experience, merchandising and promotional ability and experience, comprehensive line of packaged grocery products, ability to command consumer acceptance of its products, power to command premium shelf space in grocery stores, and ability to concentrate the full impact of its advertising, promotional, and merchandising experience and ability on one of its products or on one selected section of the country.

### ACQUISITION OF A CUSTOMER'S ASSETS

Forward vertical integration through the purchase of the assets of the would-be customer firm avoids the necessity of having to compete for that customer's business. A seller will not have to engage in price competition to obtain that business, and it will not have to maintain a sales force to do that selling. "Competition is never more irrevocably eliminated than by buying the customer for whose business the industry has been competing."[9]

Forward integration is accomplished for other reasons than simply to avert the competition for customers' business. A manufacturer may be attempting to market a new product and distribution outlets may be slow to accept it, or the flow of product through independent wholesale outlets may prove irregular. A quick way to break up such distribution bottlenecks is to buy up distribution outlets. Also, this is a quicker method than constructing new facilities. And it may be relatively easy to finance if an exchange of stock can be arranged. Thus a plywood specialty manufacturer, having difficulties in getting independent jobbers to carry the company's particular line of products, exchanged stock with two companies with the result that the manufacturer gained control over thirty-five warehouse outlets.[10]

[9] Justice Douglas in his dissenting opinion in *United States v. Columbia Steel Co.,* 334 U.S. 495, 537 (1948).
[10] *Business Week,* Aug. 4, 1962, p. 48.

Backward integration into manufacturing is the other side of the coin from forward integration into distribution. A distributor may buy up the firm from which it receives supplies; that supplier, however, now has an automatic source of sales. Where seller and buyer come together and effect a merger, it is not always clear which party to the transaction was most anxious to effect the integration.

Vertical integration is not illegal per se. The relevant Federal statutory provision is Section 7 of the Clayton Act as amended in 1950. It is specific about the acquisition of assets, and only an incipient or probable injurious effect upon competition need be found in order to condemn a merger. Only about a dozen cases involving a purely vertical relationship have been brought by the two Federal enforcement agencies under this 1950 act, but the first case under this act to be decided by the Supreme Court included vertical as well as horizontal integration aspects. This was the Brown Shoe case, decided in 1962.[11]

The particular vertical relationship present in the Brown Shoe case was one reason to condemn the merger of a shoe manufacturer with a shoe retailer. The Brown Shoe Company, the fourth largest shoe manufacturer, accounting for about 4 per cent of the national output of shoes, merged with G. R. Kinney Corporation, accounting for only 0.5 per cent. Brown Shoe owned or controlled through franchises or agreements some 1,230 retail outlets; Kinney operated some 400 outlets, but represented the largest family-style shoe-store chain in the United States. The Kinney retail stores sold only 1.2 per cent of all national retail shoe sales by dollar volume, but the annual retail sales exceeded $42 million. However, Kinney's manufacturing plants supplied Kinney's retail outlets with only 20 per cent of their shoes. This was the crux of the decision against the vertical aspects of the merger. Brown Shoe, which had been supplying none of its manufactured products to Kinney retail outlets, conceded that to supply Kinney stores was among its reasons for the merger. The court held that this merger, as part of a trend toward vertical integration in the shoe industry, would foreclose competition

---

[11] *Brown Shoe Co., Inc. v. United States*, 370 U.S. 294 (1962).

from a substantial share of the markets for men's, women's, and children's shoes.

Section 7 forbids only those mergers which substantially lessen competition or tend to create a monopoly "in any line of commerce in any section of the country." A preliminary determination must, therefore, be made about the relevant market before a determination can be made about the effect on competition. This determination must be made with respect to both the product market and the geographic market. The Supreme Court in the Brown Shoe decision pointed out that the outer boundaries of a product market are determined by the cross-elasticity of demand between the product itself and the substitutes for it; that is, the degree of effect a small change in the price of a product will have upon the quantity demanded of the substitute products or, as the court put it, the reasonable interchangeability of use between the products. Within this broad market, said the court, "well-defined submarkets may exist, which, in themselves, constitute product markets for antitrust purposes." It then listed seven indicia for such submarkets: (1) the industry or public recognition of the market as a separate economic entity, (2) the product's peculiar characteristics and uses, (3) unique production facilities, (4) distinct customers, (5) distinct prices, (6) sensitivity to price changes, and (7) specialized vendors. Added the court:

> Because §7 of the Clayton Act prohibits any merger which may substantially lessen competition "in *any* line of commerce" (emphasis supplied), it is necessary to examine the effects of a merger in each such economically significant submarket to determine if there is a reasonable probability that the merger will substantially lessen competition. If such a probability is found to exist, the merger is proscribed.[12]

The relevant geographic market can be the nation or any part of the nation. Product value, bulk, weight, and consumer demand are pertinent in determining the relevant geographic market, said the court.

These indicia, for both the product and geographic markets, are crucial in determining whether a vertical merger is to be prohibited. The Brown Shoe case was decided on the basis of mar-

[12] 370 U.S. 294, 325 (1962).

kets for men's, women's, and children's shoes, the nation as a whole being the relevant geographic market. Brown Shoe claimed that the product market was defined too broadly, that it failed to recognize sufficiently "price/quality" and "age/sex" distinctions in shoes. It argued that it manufactured predominantly medium-priced shoes while Kinney sold mostly low-priced shoes. But the Supreme Court held that such a further breakdown of the product market would not affect the vertical results of the merger because Brown Shoe manufactured and Kinney sold comparable quantities of virtually every type of men's, women's, and children's shoes.

Three cases decided right after the Brown Shoe decision point up the significance of determining the relevant market. In the first case the Supreme Court voided the decision of a district court which had ruled that the acquisition of the Sierra Drawn Steel Corporation, a seller of cold finished steel bars, by Bliss & Laughlin, the first in the United States in terms of capacity to produce cold finished steel bars, did not violate Section 7. Said the Supreme Court: "The judgment is vacated and the case is remanded for reconsideration in the light of *Brown Shoe Co., Inc., v. United States.*"[13] The district court had ruled that there was not the requisite showing of a probability of substantial lessening of competition because the relevant geographic market was not the four-state area of California, Washington, Oregon, and Arizona as the government contended; a substantial tonnage of the product was shipped into that four-state area.[14] Receiving the case on remand, the district court found no additional evidence offered and adhered to its original decision.[15]

The second case involved the acquisition of an aluminum foil converting firm by Reynolds Metals Company. The acquired company, Arrow Brands, Inc., converted aluminum foil to sell it nationally to wholesale florist-supply houses for decorative purposes. A court of appeals upheld a Federal Trade Commission order against the acquisition.[16] At issue in the case was the

[13] *United States v. Bliss & Laughlin, Inc.,* 83 Sup. Ct. 156 (1962).

[14] 202 F. Supp. 335 (1962).

[15] Trade Reg. Rep., par. 70,734 (So. Cal. 1963).

[16] *Reynolds Metals Co. v. Federal Trade Commission,* 309 F.2d 223 (1962)

"relevant line of commerce." Reynolds challenged the Commission's selection of the sale of decorative aluminum foil to the florist trade on the basis of "peculiar characteristics and uses" as being determinative of the relevant product market. The court agreed with Reynolds on this point, but nevertheless upheld the Commission on the relevant product market on the basis of three other indicia: public and industrial recognition of the product as a separate economic entity, its distinct customers, and its distinct prices. Having narrowed the relevant market down to eight relatively small independent *florist* foil converters (against all types of producers and sellers of colored or embossed aluminum foil), it was not too difficult to find an injurious impact on competition. Arrow, which had about 33 per cent of the market before the acquisition, was now being backed by the power of the "deep pocket" or "rich parent," said the court, and this "opened the possibility and power to sell at prices approximating cost or below and thus to undercut and ravage the less affluent competition." This showing of "capacity or potentiality to lessen competition" was enough to condemn. The court noted further, however, an *actual* anticompetitive effect. Arrow had cut prices retroactively after having been acquired, resulting in a significant shift of business away from five of Arrow's competitors.

In the third case a district court failed to support the government's charge that the acquisition of Rome Cable Corporation by the Aluminum Company of America was illegal. Rome Cable produced aluminum and copper wire and cable. The Department of Justice had broken the product market down into ten submarkets based upon the peculiar characteristics and uses test and held an eleven-state area to be the relevant geographic market. The district court disagreed, holding first, that the wire and cables in issue were largely interchangeable and second, that the nation as a whole was the pertinent geographic market. Having broadened the markets, the court could see no substantial lessening of competition.[17]

---

[17] *United States v. Aluminum Company of America and Rome Cable Corp.*, 214 F. Supp. 501 (1963). This decision was reversed by the Supreme Court in June, 1964.

## ACQUISITION OF A CUSTOMER'S CAPITAL STOCK

One method to control sales is to acquire a sufficient percentage of a customer's capital stock to influence the buying policy of that customer. The original Section 7 of the Clayton Act of 1914, which referred only to the acquisition of the capital stock of a corporation, remained largely dormant for years because the stock which was being acquired could skirt possible legal attack by being quickly used to purchase the corporation's assets. Once the assets were acquired, it was too late to bring suit under the act.[18] This loophole was not closed until the 1950 amendment to the Clayton Act, which brought the acquisition of assets as well as that of stock within the purview of the act. But the un-amended Section 7 proved to be a "sleeping giant," for it was eventually awakened by the Department of Justice filing a complaint in 1949 and successfully suing to force du Pont to give up the voting stock which it held in the General Motors Corporation.

Where the holdings of the stock of another corporation represent more than 50 per cent of that other corporation's stock, then the held corporation may well be looked upon as a subsidiary company which is a part of the mother (holding) company's complex or group. But where the holdings of the stock of another corporation represent considerably less than half the outstanding capital shares of that corporation, it may be difficult to discover whether those holdings are for purposes of or have the effect of control, or are simply an investment. Many corporations hold stock in other corporations purely for investment purposes, and Section 7, both the old and the amended, specifically exempts stock purchased "solely for investment and not using the same by voting or otherwise to bring about, or in attempting to bring about, the substantial lessening of competition."

This was the primary issue in the du Pont-General Motors case. Did the 23 per cent stock interest (63 million shares) of General Motors held by du Pont simply represent an invest-

---

[18] *Thatcher Manufacturing Co. v. Federal Trade Commission*, 272 U.S. 554 (1926).

ment, or was this an effective device by which du Pont became a principal supplier to General Motors under conditions free from market competition? The district court dismissed the government action, finding no restraint on trade.[19] When the case was appealed to the Supreme Court, du Pont argued that the unamended Section 7 applied only to horizontal, and not to vertical, acquisitions. The high court, making its first ruling on this point, held that it applied to any acquisition. Furthermore, the Supreme Court decided in favor of the government,[20] eventually requiring that an order be fashioned which would require du Pont to dispose of all its General Motors shares within ten years.[21]

The amount of business that flowed to du Pont from General Motors was large; in 1947 total purchases amounted to over $26 million. Du Pont supplied 67 per cent of General Motors' requirements for finishes in 1946 and 68 per cent in 1947. With respect to General Motors' fabric requirements, du Pont supplied over 52 per cent in 1946 and over 38 per cent in 1947. This represented a substantial portion of the automobile industry's requirements for such products since General Motors accounted for almost one-half of that industry's annual sales. This was the market which was considered relevant. The court rejected the argument that the total finishes and fabrics markets were the relevant market.

To return to our basic question: Was du Pont's stock investment in General Motors purely an investment and thus exempt from the statute? The highest court saw du Pont's influence brought to bear to make du Pont a primary supplier to General Motors. In the words of the court:

We agree with the trial court that considerations of price, quality and service were not overlooked by either du Pont or General Motors. Pride in its products and its high financial stake in General Motors' success would naturally lead du Pont to try to supply the best. But the wisdom of this business judgment cannot obscure the fact, plainly revealed by the record, that du Pont purposely employed its stock to pry open the General Motors mar-

[19] *United States v. E. I. du Pont de Nemours and Co. et al.,* 126 F. Supp. 235 (1954).
[20] 353 U.S. 586 (1957).
[21] 366 U.S. 316 (1961).

ket to entrench itself as the primary supplier of General Motors' requirements for automotive finishes and fabrics.

Similarly, the fact that all concerned in high executive posts in both
companies acted honorably and fairly, each in the honest conviction that his
actions were in the best interests of his own company and without any design
to overreach anyone, including du Pont's competitors, does not defeat the
Government's right to relief. It is not requisite to the proof of a violation of
Section 7 to show that restraint or monopoly was intended.[22]

It should be clear from these words that the acquisition of
the stock of any customer where a sizable portion of a particular
product of an industry is involved is suspect as violating the law.
And lest any business firms feel secure that they are not violating
the law because their stock acquisitions occurred at some time
in the distant past, it should be noted that the Supreme Court
said that the "incipiency" of the restraint does not just occur at
the time of the acquisition; it can occur at any time after the
acquisition. Thus an acquisition of stock solely for investment
may become tainted "at any time the stock is used to bring about
or in attempting to bring about the substantial lessening of
competition."[23]

### THE JOINT VENTURE

Buyer-seller relationships in the marketplace can assume many
guises. One of these is the joint venture. This corporate relationship, in which one corporation is owned jointly by two or more
corporations, has been utilized for several years in such industries as petroleum, petrochemicals, glass, and iron and steel. It
provides a means to pool capital and resources and to share risk.
The function of marketing may help account for the formation
of a joint venture. Indeed, the first joint venture to be tested in
court under Section 7 of the Clayton Act involved the production
and *marketing* of a chemical product.

When Olin Mathieson Chemical Corporation and Pennsalt
Chemicals Corporation formed a jointly owned corporation,
Penn-Olin Chemical Company, to produce and sell sodium
chlorate, the Department of Justice challenged the joint venture.
The acquisition by the two companies of the stock of the cor-

22 353 U.S. 586, 606–607 (1957).
23 *Ibid.*, 597–598.

poration of their own creation violated Section 7 and the combination and pooling of resources violated Section 1 of the Sherman Act, stated the complaint. A district court held the joint venture to be legal; but the Supreme Court remanded the case for further evidence.[24]

Prior to the acquisition Olin Mathieson was not a producer but a large buyer of sodium chlorate. It occupied a leading position in the technology of sodium chlorate applications. Pennsalt, on the other hand, was a leading producer; it and two other companies accounted for virtually all the production of the product in the country. Olin, however, was not a customer of Pennsalt. Pennsalt's production facilities were in the West. A basic question for Pennsalt was how it might sell in substantial volume in the southeastern part of the country, which had the highest concentration of buyers. Its answer was to build a plant in Kentucky jointly with Olin and use the sales force which Olin already had established in the Southeast.

The Department of Justice claimed that the joint venture would eliminate the *potential* competition between Pennsalt and Olin Mathieson in the production of sodium chlorate because Olin would not now consider producing that product on its own. It would eliminate actual competition between them with respect to other chemicals because they would have the opportunity to make agreements when they were convened for the joint venture purposes. And Olin would be eliminated as a buyer of sodium chlorate from Pennsalt's competitors.

The lower court rejected the government position. There was no evidence that the two companies would have built separate plants to produce sodium chlorate if they had not entered the joint venture. To provide the opportunity for collusion with respect to other chemicals is not the same thing as collusion itself. And as for Olin's buying its sodium chlorate from Penn-Olin rather than from other suppliers, the court saw strong competition from two larger suppliers. Indeed, the joint venture was the means to break into a market, not to preempt it, and to challenge the supremacy of two companies which were domi-

---

[24] *United States v. Penn-Olin Chemical Co. et al.,* Trade Reg. Rep., par. 70,762 (Del., 1963); Sup. Ct., June, 1964.

nating it. We can see from this case that there is more than one pair of glasses through which a market situation can be viewed.

## RECIPROCITY

Business "reciprocity" is a practice which has come under antitrust scrutiny. Reciprocity is represented by the situation in which sales by one firm are facilitated by the fact that the buyer is also a seller of goods to that firm from which it buys. Seller A can sell to buyer B not just on the basis of market competition, but also because buyer B is anxious to sell his products or services to seller A. If there is a certain degree of inequality of bargaining power, which may derive from the relative size of the firms involved, market power in the selling effort may be exerted. If so, the guardians of antitrust may attack.

The Federal Trade Commission issued three cease and desist orders under Section 5 of the Federal Trade Commission Act against the practice of reciprocity in the 1930s. Two of these orders involved the control over rail shipments of meat by meat packers to induce railroads to purchase certain items of railroad equipment from companies in which officials of the meat-packing companies had an interest.[25] A third order involved a large food packer which was using its buying power in the purchase of raw materials for its canning operations and also of manufactured products to induce the sellers to use rail and ship terminal facilities owned by it.[26]

Cease and desist orders do not reach to the heart of the power of reciprocity, and efforts directed against reciprocity in the early 1960s have sought divestiture of certain corporate divisions. The Department of Justice highlighted the coercive element in reciprocity in the criminal action which it filed against General Motors under Section 2 of the Sherman Act in 1961.[27] General Motors was indicted by a Federal grand jury on charges of using its vast economic power to monopolize the manufacture and sale of railroad locomotives. The government charged that

[25] *Waugh Equipment Co. et al.*, 15 F.T.C. 232 (1931); *Mechanical Manufacturing Co. et al.*, 16 F.T.C. 67 (1932).

[26] *California Packing Corp. et al.*, 25 F.T.C. 379 (1937).

[27] *United States v. General Motors Corp.*, Criminal Action 61–CR–356, Apr. 12, 1961.

the sale of locomotives was influenced when General Motors routed rail shipments of its own products to favor those railroads which purchased General Motors locomotives and withheld rail shipments from the railroads which purchased locomotives from General Motors competitors. The result of this reciprocity was, according to the government, that two substantial competitors were driven from the market, allowing General Motors to capture 84.1 per cent of the railroad locomotive business. A parallel civil suit filed in 1963, charging violations of Section 2 of the Sherman Act and Section 7 of the Clayton Act, sought the divestiture by General Motors of its Electro-Motive Division and other assets necessary to establish that division as an independent manufacturer.[28]

The Department of Justice has also charged an illegal use of market power to ensure reciprocity in its 1962 complaint against General Dynamics Corporation.[29] At that time General Dynamics was the nation's largest defense contractor. It used this power as a lever to force firms which sold to it to buy their carbon dioxide and other industrial gas requirements from it; this was a claimed violation of Section 1 of the Sherman Act. In 1957 General Dynamics had acquired a carbon dioxide producer, Liquid Carbonic Corporation, and as a result General Dynamics came to account for 29 per cent of domestic sales of carbon dioxide, not counting the amount of the product it produced for its own use. This acquisition, claimed the government, represented a violation of Section 7 of the Clayton Act—through reciprocity, independent carbon dioxide sellers were being excluded from the market. The government asked that General Dynamics divest itself of its carbon dioxide division.

The Federal Trade Commission ruled in 1962 against a merger which it charged contributed to reciprocity.[30] In this case Consolidated Foods Corporation, a large processor, wholesaler, and retailer of food, acquired in 1951 Gentry, Inc., a manufacturer of dried food seasonings, including dehydrated onion

[28] *United States v. General Motors Corp.,* Civil Action 63C80, Jan. 14, 1963.

[29] *United States v. General Dynamics Corp.,* Civil Action 62C3686, Nov. 8, 1962.

[30] *Consolidated Foods Corp.,* Federal Trade Commission Docket 7000.

and garlic. Consolidated purchases the products of many food processors, who, in packing their foods, require this dehydrated onion and garlic. Food processors, using these ingredients and anxious to make sales to Consolidated, are certain to be under some pressure to buy their dehydrated onion and garlic supplies from Consolidated's Gentry Division. The merger, the Commission claimed, gave Consolidated the power to extort or attract reciprocal purchases from suppliers. Gentry had thus acquired a protected market which would deny fair competitive opportunities to other smaller, and relatively undiversified, sellers of these dehydrated products, and entry would be discouraged. Consolidated admitted exercising this power, expressly conditioning its purchases from processors on their purchases from Gentry. But the Commission utilized Section 7 of the Clayton Act to attack this acquisition partly because, even if the reciprocity was not presently overt and even though Consolidated may not have thus far severely impaired competition, the merger had given Consolidated the power to foreclose competition and impair it whenever it might choose to do so in the future. A circuit court of appeals, however, reversed the Federal Trade Commission's decision, holding that whereas Consolidated's share of the dehydrated onion market increased by 7 per cent, its share of the dehydrated garlic market sustained a decrease of 12 per cent. The Commission had erred, said the court, in rejecting this record in favor of a "future possibility based on conjecture and speculation."[31]

## EXCLUSIVE DEALING

One means of distribution available to a manufacturer is to have an agreement with the distributors under which the distributors agree to handle only the products of that manufacturer, or, similarly, not to handle products of competitors. Such agreements represent exclusive dealing. They may involve manufacturers and wholesalers, manufacturers and retailers, wholesalers and retailers, or other possible relationships. In essence, the arrangement represents contractual forward integration.

---

[31] *Consolidated Foods Corp. v. Federal Trade Commission,* Trade Reg. Rep., par. 71,054 (C.A.–7, 1964).

Selling under exclusive dealing arrangements may carry with it certain advantages to, and therefore be desired by, both the seller and the buyer. From the seller's point of view, selling and promotional and perhaps even production expenses are reduced, for the goods flow to the distributor automatically and with more predictability than would be true in an open market. As compared with a manufacturer's owning and operating these distribution facilities, exclusive dealing saves the manufacturer the necessity of making this capital investment. The seller is also likely to find that the buyer, specializing in one brand of goods, will take a direct and personal interest in the goodwill attached to the manufacturer's brand name or trademark and promote the goods accordingly. All these advantages of an exclusive dealing arrangement may be of crucial importance to the relatively small competitor attempting to secure a position in the marketplace against larger competitors.

From the buyer's point of view, an exclusive dealing arrangement makes the source of supply more certain, a matter which assumes special importance during periods of shortage. Also, deliveries can be made by the supplier automatically, just as deliveries of heating oil are made to the residential consumer. Dealing in only one brand of good eliminates the need to carry the large inventories which are necessary when several different brands are stocked. And, if the goods handled are machines which require maintenance, dealing in only one type reduces technical "know-how" requirements.

A by-product of a dealer's agreement to deal exclusively in the products of one manufacturer is that other manufacturers are excluded from selling to that dealer. Yet exclusive dealing is not illegal per se. Section 3 of the Clayton Act makes these agreements about conditions of sale illegal only where the result may be a substantial lessening of competition or a tendency to create a monopoly. Essentially, the legality of the arrangement depends upon whether the market power has resulted in exclusion of competitors from a substantial market or whether the arrangement was freely entered by both parties to serve a useful economic function. The Supreme Court's 1961 Tampa Electric decision, based on Section 3, tells us that we must look at the facts in each case and balance the good and bad effects produced by the contract. More specifically, the court listed as factors to be considered: (1) the type of goods or merchandise, (2) the geographic area of effective competition, and (3) the substantiality of the competition foreclosed.[32]

Contracts in the oil industry requiring retail service stations to handle the supplies (motor oil, tires, batteries, and accessories, as well as gasoline) of one major oil company exclusively have been condemned under Section 3 as a "potential clog on competition."[33] Since all the major oil refiners engaged in the same practice, it was a system foreclosing other suppliers from this market. Such exclusive dealing in the oil industry is illegal as well under oral agreements[34] or under understandings brought about by sales persuasion and possible loss of a supply source.[35] In the dress-pattern industry, Standard Fashion Company's prohibition of the use of competitors' patterns by its retailers was found to violate Section 3 because Standard Fashion controlled 40 per cent of the business and the exclusive dealing arrangements would lead only toward further concentration in the industry as competitors were excluded by this dominant seller.[36] In the auto-parts industry, an independent seller of carburetors for the replacement market was held to occupy such a dominant position (30 per cent) and such a complete line in that market that no service station could successfully carry on its business without carrying some of that seller's products; an exclusive dealing requirement, therefore, foreclosed competitors to such a degree as to violate Section 3.[37]

Cases can also be cited in which exclusive dealing was found not to violate Section 3 of the Clayton Act. An automobile manufacturer required dealers to sell only parts produced by that manufacturer. When the record showed that competition in

[32] *Tampa Electric Co. v. Nashville Coal Co.*, 365 U.S. 320, 327–329 (1961).

[33] *Standard Oil Co. of California et al. v. United States*, 337 U.S. 293, 314 (1949).

[34] *United States v. Richfield Oil Corp.*, 99 F. Supp. 280 (1951), *affirmed per curiam*, 343 U.S. 922 (1952).

[35] *United States v. Sun Oil Co.*, 176 F. Supp. 715 (1959).

[36] *Standard Fashion Co. v. Magrane-Houston Co.*, 258 U.S. 346 (1922).

[37] *Carter Carburetor Corp. v. Federal Trade Commission*, 112 F.2d 722 (1940).

the sale of auto replacement parts had substantially increased throughout the period of time involved in the case, the court could see no substantial lessening of competition under Section 3.[38] J. I. Case Company, the farm-machinery manufacturer, emphasized to its dealers that it desired them to devote the major part of their activities to the Case line of equipment. The court could not see an adverse effect on competition because there was no showing that farm-machinery manufacturers had difficulty in obtaining dealers and there was an adequate number of full-line and short-line manufacturers represented in most towns in agricultural areas.[39]

Section 5 of the Federal Trade Commission Act has also been utilized by the Commission against exclusive dealing, the Commission charging that the practice can be an unfair method of competition as well as a method of distribution which may substantially lessen competition. Section 5 has thus accompanied Section 3 charges in complaints and cease and desist orders in the distribution of such goods as kitchenware,[40] cosmetics,[41] and hearing aids.[42]

The right of a seller to select his own customers provides the seller with a possible avenue of escape from a charge of exclusive dealing. If a seller feels that exclusive dealing is necessary in order for a dealer to provide him with "adequate representation" of his product, then he can refuse to deal, or perhaps refuse to renew a contract or franchise, with those dealers who do not devote sufficient attention to selling his products. In this way perhaps close to 100 per cent exclusive dealing can be achieved. But no coercion or intimidation can be used against the dealer to ensure exclusive dealing.[43] Nor can any refusal to deal be part of an attempt or conspiracy to restrain trade or monopolize.

---

[38] *Pick Mfg. Co. v. General Motors Corp.*, 80 F.2d 641 (1935), *affirmed per curiam*, 299 U.S. 3 (1936).

[39] *United States v. J. I. Case Company*, 101 F. Supp. 856 (1951).

[40] *National Pressure Cooker Co. et al.*, 45 F.T.C. 294 (1948).

[41] *Duon, Inc. and Donald H. Miller*, 48 F.T.C. 790 (1952).

[42] *Dictograph Products, Inc.*, 50 F.T.C. 281 (1953), *affirmed*, 217 F.2d 821 (1954).

[43] The purpose of the passage of the Automobile Dealer Franchise Act of 1956 was to give an automobile dealer an opportunity to bring suits to recover damages when the manufacturer does not act in good faith in com-

## REQUIREMENTS CONTRACTS

One variant of exclusive dealing is the requirements contract. Under such a contract the buyer agrees to purchase all or a part of his requirements of a product from one seller, usually for a specified period of time. Such a contract ensures for the seller a fairly definite amount of business over a definite period of time in the future. For the buyer the principal advantage is that concern over a source of supply is minimized.

Requirements contracts may violate either the Sherman Act or Section 3 of the Clayton Act. The American Can Company was found to restrain trade unreasonably in violation of the Sherman Act when it required food-processing lessees of its can-closing machinery to buy all their supply of cans on five-year contracts.[44] American Can was able to insist on these requirements contracts because it controlled patents on certain can-closing machinery and it leased this machinery at such low rentals that the lessees could not afford not to lease the machinery. The result, however, was to erect a formidable barrier to other sellers of cans. In a second case, Richfield Oil Company was found to be in violation of both Section 1 of the Sherman Act and Section 3 of the Clayton Act when it required its lessee service stations to purchase all their petroleum products and accessories from Richfield.[45] Richfield ensured acquiescence with such requirements through a twenty-four-hour termination clause in the service-station lease. Illegality rested, it will be noted in both these cases, on some power the seller held over the buyer.

Requirements contracts are not always illegal, however. The contract of a seller of bituminous coal to supply the total requirements of an electric-power utility company in Florida for twenty years was found not to violate Section 3 even though the contract involved an average of 1 million tons a year.[46] The

plying with the terms of a franchise or in terminating or not renewing a franchise. A lack of good faith is determined under this act in a context of coercion or intimidation.

[44] *United States v. American Can Co. et al.,* 87 F. Supp. 18 (1949).

[45] *United States v. Richfield Oil Corp.,* 99 F. Supp. 280 (1951), *affirmed per curiam,* 343 U.S. 922 (1952).

[46] *Tampa Electric Co. v. Nashville Coal Co.,* 365 U.S. 320 (1961).

*supplier* of coal wanted to get out of this long-term contract and claimed that it was an illegal contract. But the Supreme Court held that the amount of coal business involved represented only 0.77 per cent of the coal produced and sold in the relevant coal-producing region, and this did not represent a substantial lessening of competition.

### EXCLUSIVE TERRITORIAL DISTRIBUTORSHIPS

Exclusive dealing has aspects other than that of confining distributors to the products of only one supplier. A manufacturer may designate and assign a certain geographic territory to one distributor, agreeing not to sell to any other distributors in that region. Or the manufacturer may have an agreement with the distributor that the latter confine his sales to that geographic region.

Where the manufacturer agrees not to sell to any other distributor in a given area, the distributor is protected to a large degree from the competition of rivals supplied by the same manufacturer. Such an arrangement provides inducement to distributors to handle and actively promote that manufacturer's products. Where the agreement confines the distributor to sales within the defined geographic region, the manufacturer also feels that he is encouraging the distributor to develop his own territory to the fullest, for the distributors will not be able to raid each other's territories in their sales efforts.

Both of these arrangements supplement each other, but there is a basic difference between the two. In the first, the manufacturer is only selecting his own customers in a fashion which he deems will maximize the sales effort of his distributors. In the second, the result is the same as if the distributors had joined together and agreed to divide the market up among themselves and not compete with each other.

In spite of the implicit market sharing inherent in the restriction by manufacturers of distributors' sales efforts to their own geographical territory, such an arrangement is not illegal per se under the Sherman Act. In its 1963 White Motor decision the Supreme Court, in its first decision involving a territorial restriction in a *vertical* arrangement,[47] refused to accept a dis-

---

[47] *The White Motor Co. v. United States,* 83 Sup. Ct. 696 (1963).

trict court's decision that such an arrangement was illegal per se.[48] The lower court's decision had been made on the basis of a summary judgment without full trial, and the Supreme Court remanded the case back to the district court in order to learn "of the economic and business stuff out of which these arrangements emerge." It may be, suggested the court, that the restraint on intrabrand competition fostered more effective interbrand competition. Was this the manufacturer's desire and intent? Or was it the distributors who forced the manufacturer to assign the exclusive territories in order to eliminate the competition among the distributors?

Since the Supreme Court in its White Motor decision did not come out and clearly state that a rule of reason should be applied to such territorial restriction arrangements, it has been argued that it did not say that such arrangements are not illegal per se. Yet the Seventh Circuit Court of Appeals four months later, in a decision overturning a Federal Trade Commission order which had condemned such an arrangement under Section 5 of the Federal Trade Commission Act, stated that the Supreme Court did say in its decision that vertical allocations of dealer territory are not per se violations of the Sherman Act.[49]

## TYING ARRANGEMENTS

A tying arrangement is one in which a seller sells one product, the "tying" product, only on condition that the buyer also purchase another, the "tied" product. Where leverage power resides in the tying product, it can be used to facilitate sales of another product. Where this power is used by a seller to force a buyer to purchase his whole line of goods, the arrangement is known as "full-line forcing." Tie-in sales are always subject to the possibility of being found illegal under Section 3 of the Clayton Act and/or under the Sherman Act. For other sellers may be denied free access to the market for the tied product and buyers may be forced to forego their free choice between competing products.

International Business Machines was not permitted to force

[48] 194 F. Supp. 562 (1961).
[49] *Snap-On Tools Corporation v. Federal Trade Commission,* 321 F.2d 825, 828 (1963).

the lessees of its automatic tabulating machines to purchase their tabulating cards from it. For there were only two companies leasing such machines, and other companies were capable of producing cards which performed satisfactorily in these machines.[50] International Salt Company was not permitted to tie the sale of salt (unpatented) to the lease of salt-dispensing machines (patented) where the amount of business involved was considered substantial (119,000 tons). Said the court: "It is unreasonable, per se, to foreclose competitors from any substantial market."[51] And the Automatic Canteen Company of America was prohibited from tying in the sale of candy products with the leasing of automatic vending machines, of which there were more than 200,000 in operation. "This constitutes a very substantial interference with competition."[52]

The Supreme Court said in 1953 in its Times-Picayune decision that tying contracts are illegal per se under Section 3 of the Clayton Act where the seller enjoys a monopolistic position in the market for the tying product *or* if a substantial volume of commerce in the tied product is restrained. The court went on to say that to violate Section 1 of the Sherman Act, however, *both* of these conditions must be met.[53] Then in 1958 the Supreme Court in its Northern Pacific Railway decision said that tying agreements are unreasonable per se under Section 1 of the Sherman Act if the seller has "sufficient economic power" with respect to the tying product to appreciably restrain trade in the tied product.[54] Nevertheless, in spite of the reference to per se illegality, it is still necessary to determine when such conditions of economic power exist. When the tying product is patented, there is no doubt some element of monopoly. And a court in a Section 3 case has held that a patent on the tying product supplies, prima facie or per se, the monopolistic element necessary

---

[50] *International Business Machines Corp. v. United States,* 298 U.S. 131 (1936).

[51] *International Salt Co., Inc. v. United States,* 332 U.S. 392, 396 (1947).

[52] *Automatic Canteen Co. of America v. Federal Trade Commission,* 194 F.2d 433, 437 (1952).

[53] *Times-Picayune Publishing Co. v. United States,* 345 U.S. 594, 608–609 (1953).

[54] *Northern Pacific Railway Co. v. United States,* 356 U.S. 1, 6 (1958).

to condemn the arrangement.[55] In the Times-Picayune case itself, however, the Supreme Court said that the necessary monopoly did not exist. The newspaper *Times-Picayune* published both a morning and an evening edition in New Orleans. It had a competitor only for the evening edition. It refused to sell advertising space in the morning edition alone; advertisers had to purchase space in the evening edition as well. One might presume that the morning edition was used as the tying product to sell space in the evening edition. But the Supreme Court held the relevant market to be the whole day with its three newspapers, and therefore, the monopoly power of a tying product was not present.

In theory, where no leverage exists in a product, there can be no tying arrangement by coercion—the buyer can always go elsewhere to purchase. Even a patent may not provide any real leverage; the patentee may hold a patent monopoly, but that patent may have no real monopoly power in the marketplace. But where there is any significant leverage, there can be some element of pressure to force a buyer to purchase a tied product, to the exclusion of other sellers. Exactly what degree of monopoly power and of leverage is necessary to condemn a tying arrangement, however, remains somewhat uncertain.

## SUGGESTIONS FOR FURTHER READING

For analysis of government policy toward mergers, see Betty Bock, *Mergers and Markets*, 2d ed., National Industrial Conference Board, New York, 1962, and Joel B. Dirlam, "The Celler-Kefauver Act: A Review of Enforcement Policy," *Administered Prices: A Compendium on Public Policy*, Subcommittee on Antitrust and Monopoly of the Senate Committee on the Judiciary, 88th Cong., 1st Sess., 1963. For data on acquisitions by company, 1951 through 1961, see *Mergers and Superconcentration: Acquisitions of 500 Largest Industrial and 50 Largest Merchandising Firms, Staff Report of the House Select Committee on Small Business*, 87th Cong., 2d Sess., 1962.

Discussion of various aspects of forward contractual integration can be found in Kenneth J. Curran, "Exclusive Dealing and Public Policy," *Journal of Marketing*, October, 1950; Donald F. Turner, "The Validity of Tying Arrangements under the Antitrust Laws," *Harvard Law Review*, November,

---

[55] *United States v. American Linen Supply Co.*, 141 F. Supp. 105, 112 (1956).

1958; note in the *Harvard Law Review,* February, 1962, on "Restricted Channels of Distribution"; and Carl Kaysen, *United States v. United Shoe Machinery Corporation,* Harvard University Press, Cambridge, Mass., 1956.

For opposing points of view on the du Pont-General Motors decision, see J. B. Dirlam and I. M. Stelzer, "The du Pont-General Motors Decision: In the Antitrust Grain," *Columbia Law Review,* January, 1958; and Alfred Nicols, "Economic Issues in the du Pont-General Motors Case," *Journal of Business,* July, 1960.

Comments on reciprocity are made by W. F. Mueller and G. W. Stocking, "Business Reciprocity and the Size of Firms," *Journal of Business,* April, 1957; and by William M. Carley, "Swapping Business," *Wall Street Journal,* Dec. 4, 1963.

# 5

# ADVERTISING AND LABELING

Advertising and labeling are inherent parts of the marketing process. The consumer is clearly not all-knowledgeable. He needs to be informed. Products vary from manufacturer to manufacturer not only according to price but also according to durability, workability, eye appeal, and so on. It thus behooves the seller to make the buyer fully aware of the nature and advantages of his wares. This is an important part of competition. The more fully informed the buyer is, the more intelligent his market decisions will be.

Much ink has been spilt over the question of the overall success of advertising in serving the economy. Some argue that excessive amounts are being spent on advertising, that prices are being kept too high as a result, that the consumer is being persuaded to purchase goods he does not really need or want, or that such expenditures may act as a block to entry of potential new competitors. Others argue that advertising creates markets, lowers prices, increases competition, and is vital to our economic and social growth. The law takes the position that as long as misrepresentation in advertising is prevented, then competition, and thus the consumer, will be effectively served.

The problem of preventing misrepresentation in advertising has several aspects. A marketer can frequently be seduced by the qualities and beneficial characteristics of the goods he is selling. The result is "puffing" or exaggerated praise or opinion of a product, perhaps normal for the enthusiastic salesman. Somewhere, however, the exaggeration can become a distortion which can mislead the consumer. When this occurs, the function of providing the consumer with full knowledge so that his buying decisions can be more intelligent is no longer being adequately performed. And, further, it must be admitted, the exaggeration is sometimes deliberate. The distinction between "puffing" and deliberate misrepresentation is a matter of degree. It is also a matter of intent and may be difficult to distinguish.

The public policy (legal) problem of the advertising and labeling of goods is that of preventing misrepresentations. Not only must the consumer be protected but also business must be shielded from those marketers who are either careless or lack full integrity in their advertising and labeling efforts. Our concern in this chapter will be to examine the regulatory authorities which exist and the many aspects of advertising and labeling over which the power of authority has had to be exerted in order that misrepresentation and deception be eliminated.

## AUTHORITIES FOR REGULATION OF ADVERTISING AND LABELING

False or deceptive advertising and labeling in interstate commerce are unfair methods of competition or unfair or deceptive acts or practices under Section 5 of the Federal Trade Commission Act. False or deceptive representations in newspapers, on the radio or television, in catalogs or brochures, in literature sent through the United States mail, on labels, invoices, price lists or similar printed matter, and even in sales talk, have all been held to be subject to the jurisdiction of the Federal Trade Commission under Section 5. The dissemination of false advertisements of foods, drugs, cosmetics, and therapeutic devices used in the diagnosis, treatment, or prevention of disease are specifically declared to be unlawful in Sections 12 through 15 of the act as added by the Wheeler-Lea Act of 1938. For these products "false advertisement" means an advertisement, other than labeling, which is misleading in a material respect. The unfair or deceptive labeling (as distinguished from advertising) of these products can still be reached under the broadly interpreted Section 5, however. Deceptive packaging as a form of misrepresentation can likewise be remedied through the application of Section 5. The Federal Trade Commission also administers the special laws enacted to cover the special problems of labeling present in the textile and fur industries. These acts are the Wool Products Labeling Act of 1939, the Fur Products Labeling Act of 1951, and the Textile Fiber Products Identification Act of 1958.

Misrepresentations in the *labeling* of foods, drugs, therapeutic devices, or cosmetics are subject to the jurisdiction of the Food and Drug Administration in the Department of Health, Education, and Welfare under the provisions of the Federal Food, Drug, and Cosmetic Act of 1938, as amended. This act attacks "misbranding," as well as adulteration. Misbranding occurs when the labels are "false or misleading in any particular," when the container is "made, formed, or filled as to be misleading," and when labels are not complete as to proper description of the containers' contents. The Food and Drug Administration can attack *advertising* to the degree that "labeling" by statute includes the written, printed, or graphic matter *accompanying* the products subject to its jurisdiction. This agency also enforces certain requirements pertaining to prescription drug advertising. The Food and Drug Administration also controls the labeling of hazardous substances under the provisions of the Federal Hazardous Substances Labeling Act of 1960.

Other Federal authorities exert regulatory control over advertising and labeling in specific areas. That over alcoholic beverages is supervised by the Internal Revenue Service of the Treasury Department. The Civil Aeronautics Board has the responsibility of dealing with unfair and deceptive advertising by airlines. The Securities and Exchange Commission can exert certain controls to help achieve truthfulness in the advertising of securities. The Agriculture Department is assigned the function of preventing false or misleading statements or misrepresentation by stamps, labels, or marks on perishable agricultural commodities and has jurisdiction over the false labeling and advertising of agricultural and vegetable seeds. The Secretary of the Treasury has the duty of supervising the requirement that imported goods be marked to show clearly the country of origin.

The United States Post Office authorities have means at

their disposal to prevent or remedy misrepresentation. Materials to obtain money by false or fraudulent pretenses, representations, or promises are nonmailable and will be returned to the sender marked "Fraudulent." The Postal Inspection Service of the Post Office Department can also provide grand juries with information for criminal mail-fraud cases conducted by United States attorneys in Federal courts.

Most of the states have enacted truth-in-advertising laws. *Printers' Ink,* a national weekly covering the general advertising field, first prepared a model law in 1911. In 1945 it provided the wording for a statute which has been adopted in twenty-seven states and the District of Columbia. This law makes it a misdemeanor to make any assertion, representation, or statement of fact in an advertisement which is untrue, deceptive, or misleading. But it does not declare against the omission of important information. Seventeen other states have enacted similar laws containing the condition that the false advertisement must be intended to deceive the reader or listener. Since intent is exceedingly difficult if not impossible to prove in court, these latter laws are ineffective. Indeed, all these laws are largely ineffective, for enforcement procedures usually involve the complainant in the expenditure of time and money and the risk of legal action for malicious prosecution. In addition, the actual enforcement has generally been in the hands of prosecuting attorneys who reputedly are too engrossed in other activities to pursue that kind of litigation.

Most of the states have laws which conform to a considerable degree to the Federal Food, Drug, and Cosmetic Act of 1938. The inclusion of a provision against false advertising is a principal difference between the state laws and the Federal law. In addition, a large number of states have laws relating to the adulteration, labeling, and packaging of specific foods and drugs, such as bread, cheese, eggs, and oleomargarine.

Several states have statutory provisions against bait advertising and misleading pricing. Some states have special laws controlling the advertising of goods and services such as dairy and agricultural products, insurance, securities, alcoholic beverages, dentistry, and small loans, just to mention a few. Many states have laws regulating retail installment sales contracts, especially with respect to motor vehicles, with the purpose of not only eliminating exorbitant charges but also hidden charges. Local ordinances may attempt to control deceptive advertising, such as "going-out-of-business" sales. Municipalities usually exert some control over outdoor advertising.

Control at the local level over false advertising is aided by more than 100 Better Business Bureaus throughout the nation. These institutions assist in the problem of maintaining truth and honesty in selling by programs for consumer education and by bringing deceptive advertising to the attention of the business firm in question, the advertising media, and the public. Where major infractions persist, the appropriate authority is urged to prosecute.

More indirect means of control over misleading advertising are represented by organizations such as Consumers Union, which publishes *Consumer Reports,* and Consumers' Research, which publishes *Consumers' Research Bulletin.* These nonprofit organizations test products and publish their findings, which frequently bring to light discrepancies between advertised claims and product performances. Such reports pierce through puffing as well as false advertising.

## MISREPRESENTATION UNDER SECTION 5

When is a representation considered either false or misleading under Section 5 of the Federal Trade Commission Act? The general principle adhered to is that the representation need have only the capacity or tendency to deceive.[1] This definition is considerably short of fraud, wherein a deliberate intent to deceive can be proved. The Supreme Court has stated that a finding of fraud is not necessary;[2] intent to deceive does not have to be shown on the part of the seller.[3] Indeed the Federal Trade Commission does not even have to show that someone has actually been deceived.[4] A "fair probability" of one's being deceived has

[1] *Goodman v. Federal Trade Commission,* 244 F.2d 584 (1957).
[2] *Federal Trade Commission v. Algoma Lumber Co.,* 291 U.S. 67 (1934).
[3] *Gimbel Bros., Inc. v. Federal Trade Commission,* 116 F.2d 578 (1941).
[4] *Northern Feather Work, Inc. v. Federal Trade Commission* and *Sumergrade v. Federal Trade Commission,* 234 F.2d 335 (1956); *American Life and Accident Insurance Co. v. Federal Trade Commission,* 225 F.2d 289 (1958).

been sufficient.[5] Even from the other side of the coin, if a possibly deceptive practice has become commonplace and the buyers have learned to discount the representation accordingly, it is still a misrepresentation.[6] Even if the seller is not aware of the falsity of the representation, this is still no defense.[7] In short, the interests of the public or the competitor receive first consideration. The rule of *caveat emptor* (let the buyer beware) does not prevail under Section 5.

The principle of capacity or tendency to deceive faces the marketers of goods with a difficult test. For they are often prone toward puffing, or the expression of an exaggerated or overly enthusiastic opinion about the value and qualities of their goods. Puffing in itself is not illegal. A line has to be drawn somewhere between permissible puffing and that which is not. It boils down to a matter of how far the puffing or expression of opinion is from actual fact. This determination in itself requires personal judgment combined with reference to whatever established standards may be available.

Some generalizations can be made about certain practices in advertising and labeling which are unacceptable under the law. First, the truth cannot be subverted by the use of words which represent less than the whole truth. "To tell less than the whole truth is a well-known method of deception; and he who deceives by resorting to such method cannot excuse the deception by relying upon the truthfulness per se of the partial truth by which it has been accomplished."[8] Thus, the inclusion in an advertisement for a certain brand of cigarettes of certain parts, but only certain parts, of an article appearing in the *Reader's Digest* created an entirely false and misleading impression not only of what was said in the article but also of the quality of the cigarettes in question. Second, advertisements which are capable of two meanings, one of which is false, are considered misleading. For example, a patent medicine might provide some relief, but advertisements which suggest that it is an effective treatment or

[5] *Herzfeld et al. v. Federal Trade Commission,* 140 F.2d 207 (1944).

[6] *Federal Trade Commission v. Winsted Hosiery Co.,* 258 U.S. 483 (1922).

[7] *Gimbel Bros., Inc. v. Federal Trade Commission,* 116 F.2d 578 (1941).

[8] *P. Lorillard Co. v. Federal Trade Commission,* 186 F.2d 52, 58 (1950).

a cure are a different matter.[9] Third, a method of description of a good which has acquired a secondary meaning cannot be accepted unless the secondary meaning is "as firmly anchored as the first one." The anchoring must indeed be firm, however, for the Supreme Court rejected the use of "white pine" to describe products made from the pine species known as *pinus ponderosa* although the name "white pine" had been used to describe that variety for over thirty years.[10]

Cease and desist orders are the most direct legal means by which the Federal Trade Commission controls misrepresentation. Although these orders may be in the form of consent orders, they are negative; they represent remedy rather than prevention. They order a marketer to cease using a particular word, or statement, or order of presentation of ideas. The Commission's powers are broad enough, however, to require disclosure. This disclosure may be accomplished by requiring the seller to qualify words which by themselves may be misleading. The Commission can order words, phrases, or statements to be either added or omitted.[11] In any case, the areas which have been implicated in misrepresentation are manifold.

## MISREPRESENTING THE NATURE AND STANDING OF A BUSINESS

The Federal Trade Commission has utilized Section 5 to condemn the use of words which mislead with respect to the true nature or standing of a business. The true nature of a business has been concealed by use of such words as "clinic," "cooperative," "foundation," "institute," "university," and the like. The misuse of words like "national," "Federal," or "United States" by some businesses may actually constitute a criminal offense.[12]

It has frequently been necessary to prohibit misrepresentation of a firm's financial condition, commercial rating, or volume of business. The length of time a firm has been in business is sometimes exaggerated by ignoring discontinuities in the busi-

---

[9] *Rhodes Pharmacal Co., Inc. v. Federal Trade Commission,* 208 F.2d 382 (1953).

[10] *Federal Trade Commission v. Algoma Lumber Co.,* 291 U.S. 67 (1934).

[11] *Feil v. Federal Trade Commission,* 285 F.2d 879 (1960).

[12] 18 U.S.C. 709.

ness. The prominence or success of a firm in the business community has also been exaggerated beyond the bounds of legal acceptance. Similar misrepresentations have pertained to the ability of a firm to fill orders, the size of a firm, or its location, number of plants, or facilities. A firm should not describe its business as "national" or "international" unless this is the true scope of the business. Claiming to have personnel that the business actually does not have is not permissible. Concealing affiliation with other seemingly independent companies and organizing bogus independents have also been held as unfair.

Misrepresentations with respect to the earnings or profits that can be anticipated by prospective salesmen or dealers of a product have been widespread, and the Commission has issued many orders and signed many stipulations in this area. For example: fur products—"$1,300 a week"; mushrooms—"540 per cent profit easily obtainable"; nut display warmers—"guaranteed return of 120 per cent"; rings—"$30 to $40 a day." Opportunities for graduates of study courses have frequently been excessively exaggerated, often by understating the qualifications necessary for obtaining positions within various trades or professions. Some cases have involved representing sales as being on consignment when they were not, offering sales assistance to dealers which was not truly available, and using advertisements of job offers when in reality the "employer" was trying to sell goods or services.

## MISREPRESENTING THE NATURE AND EFFECTIVENESS OF PRODUCTS

The Federal Trade Commission has often had to use the cease and desist order where the nature of products has been misrepresented by implication. The "mellow richness of pure New England maple" suggests that the product is genuine maple syrup. "Olive oil soap" suggests that the product is made entirely of olive oil. "Havana" in the name of cigars suggests that the cigars are made of Cuban tobacco. Using French words in describing a flavoring extract is highly suggestive that the extract is of French origin. Advertisements have tried to imply, by use of words or pictures, a relationship between perfumes and Paris, flower bulbs and Holland, rugs and Persia, and woolens and

Scotland. The words "homemade" or "handmade" should not be used when the goods were produced in a factory, and "custom-made" should not be used where the products are ready-made. Neither should the words "exclusive" or "unique" be used unless this is distinctly so.

The Commission has also found it necessary to intervene in cases involving the alleged effectiveness of products. Automobile motor attachments, books, various forms of cosmetics and oils, and insecticides have been especially vulnerable to use of gross exaggeration. Claims made for products which closely affect the consumer's personal life and ego, such as hair dyes, bust developers, and face creams, have been frequently distorted. The average consumer undoubtedly wishes to prolong youth, and creams which suggest that he can prevent sagging or wrinkling of the skin or regain youthful powers will attract a large market.

Certain words have been the subject of considerable litigation before the Commission because their definitions can be loosely interpreted. "Fireproof," "fire resistant," "fire-retardant," "noncombustible," and "heat resistant" bear different shades of meaning, and their free substitution one for another is not technically sound. Various germicidal properties claimed for such products as bleach, carpet washing solutions, and soaps have been questioned. The words "safe," "harmless," and "nonirritating" have been misused in advertising. Other words which have been used in misrepresentations are "washable," "leakproof," and "unbreakable."

Misrepresenting that a product meets certain official standards has been an abuse requiring cease and desist orders. Standards or requirements which have been illegally referred to have been those supposedly established by the U.S. Bureau of Standards, the Federal Trade Commission, the Pure Food and Drug Act, the Army, Navy, or Civilian Defense, and the "Government."

In a similar vein, the Commission has had to deal with many cases involving endorsements and testimonials. Some instances are outright falsehoods; others are false by implication. Approval by universities, doctors, the National Bureau of Standards, or the Armed Forces has been frequently hinted at in some direct or indirect fashion. The use of emblems, such as that of the Red Cross, suggests approval by that organization.

The true nature of contests or merchandise certificates has sometimes not been fully divulged or has not been honestly stated. A typical deception of this kind is to overstate the value of merchandise certificates furnished as prizes. The very nature of a contest, the rules governing it, or the chances of winning a prize have been misrepresented.

The Federal Trade Commission has found it necessary to issue guides on misrepresentation of two products especially. Shell homes, by definition, are not complete homes, but advertisements have sometimes suggested that they are. The combination of fear of nuclear attack on the part of the consumer coupled with his inadequate knowledge of protection requirements has opened a wide door to the dishonest promoter of fallout shelters.

Advertising claims of guarantees and warranties have required Commission interference. It has required disclosure of the full nature of guarantees, since they are not normally unconditional or unlimited. Time limitations, performance limits, and the part or parts to be guaranteed ordinarily are involved. Advertisements are sometimes open-end in one or more of these respects, simply saying "guaranteed" without saying with respect to what. The Commission has issued guides against deceptive advertising of guarantees. These guides require full disclosure of the nature and extent of the guarantee, the manner in which the guarantor will perform, and the identity of the guarantor. Special guidelines are also established on prorata adjustment of guarantees, "satisfaction or your money back" representations (e.g., after how long a time?), lifetime guarantees (whose life, the buyer's or seller's or the product's?), savings guarantees (e.g., 50 per cent, but of what?), and the conditions of making the guarantees good. Probably the most frequent abuse is to advertise a product as "guaranteed" . . . period.

The advertising of cigarettes has required considerable watchdog activity by the Commission. In the 1950s interbrand competition involved excessive claims about freedom from nicotine and tar or the health safety of smoking cigarettes. In 1955 the Commission finally issued guides for the advertising of cigarettes which announced that cigarette advertising should not refer to the physical effects of smoking, should not claim low tar or nicotine content or make such comparisons with other cigarettes when not established by competent scientific proof that the claim is true and of significance, should not refer to the effects of smoking on any part of the body, and should not represent medical approval of smoking. In addition, reliable information should support all claims of winning the volume race among smokers, testimonials should be genuine, and the marketers should not falsely or misleadingly disparage other cigarette manufacturers or their products. The 1955 guides specifically did not forbid, however, references to taste, flavor, aroma, or enjoyment. In mid-1964 the Commission issued a trade regulation rule which in 1965 would require the advertising and labeling of cigarettes to disclose "that cigarette smoking is dangerous to health and may cause death from cancer and other diseases."

False quantity statements on labels or packages is obviously an unfair method of competition; but other means of deception are more subtle. The Commission has successfully attacked slack filling of containers and has successfully terminated cases involving containers substantially larger than necessary to contain the products candy, cosmetics, detergents, and soap powders. It has condemned use of cartons marked "Giant Size" where this is clearly a distortion of reality.

## NATURE OF PRODUCTS AND DISCLOSURES REQUIRED

Certain aspects of the nature of products have frequently been left unmentioned in advertising, but are of such significance to the buyer that the very omission has been found to be illegal as an unfair method of competition under Section 5. Changes in products, their composition, danger in use, their foreign origin, second-hand nature, imperfections, the number of the product available, and the limitations of the product are cases in point.

A change in a product can be illustrated by the abridgement of books. If a book is abridged when reprinted, the publisher must clearly state the fact. Notice at the bottom of the page in small print and printed-over colors that decrease legibility is not sufficient. Deterioration in quality, like that which occurs in photographic film or fire extinguishers over time, is another illustration of changes in the product which must be fully disclosed.

Under today's modern technology and variety of synthetic products, the Commission has found it necessary from time to time to require disclosure of the composition of certain products. Various metals, plastics, and synthetic fibers give opportunity to the unscrupulous seller to capitalize on these deceptive appearances. Distinctions between gold and gold plating have been ignored in advertising. The Commission has processed over 200 orders or stipulations concerning the advertising, branding, labeling, or invoicing of products having a rayon content. It has found it necessary to publish a guide concerning shoe-content labeling and advertising. The use of simulated, imitation, and split leather; the fact that innersoles are concealed from view; and the use of processed leather (such as that simulating alligator) have required disclosure of the true nature of the product.

The Commission's guides for the advertising of automobile tires and tubes are an excellent illustration of the need for and requirement of full disclosure in advertising. What are "first-line" tires? A guide states that a manufacturer who designates his first-line tire as "Standard," "High Standard," or "Deluxe High Standard" cannot then refer to his tires of lesser quality as "Super Standard," "Supreme High Standard," "Super Deluxe High Standard," or "Premium." The number of plies in a tire must be fully disclosed; the phrase "Super 6" suggests six plies, but this may not represent the true facts. With respect to pricing, if a "list price" is referred to, it should be stated whose list price it is. The actual terms of a guarantee must be fully spelled out. Blemishes or imperfections of tires must not only be fully spelled out, but such condition must be stamped or molded onto the tires and the wrappings they come in. Finally, advertisements should not claim "skidproof" unless the tire provides absolute protection from skidding under all driving conditions.

The Tariff Act of 1930 requires that the foreign country of origin of imported articles must be marked so that the ultimate purchaser is fully aware of such origin. If the article itself cannot easily be marked, then its container must be marked. The Secretary of the Treasury sets up the necessary detailed regulations. An additional duty of 10 per cent ad valorem is imposed if the marking requirements are not met, and the article will be held in customs until properly marked and the additional duty paid. Defacing, removing, or altering these marks are criminal offenses. The Federal Trade Commission has become involved in this matter when, after rehandling in this country, the articles have lost identity as to foreign origin. Repackaging, installing foreign parts in otherwise domestic products, and further processing of imported articles, without proper identification of foreign origin, have been successfully attacked by the Commission.

## DISPARAGEMENT OF COMPETITORS

Long-standing marketing techniques, sometimes considered unethical, make comparisons which favor one's own products and disparage the products of competitors. If the statements are true, then the practice is legitimate. But any false or deceptive comparisons or disparagements are an unfair method of competition. Comparisons are unfair not only when they claim untrue superiorities but also when they claim untrue equality. They range from "superior to all similar products" to "lasts three times as long." Disparagement of competitors' products has taken several other different forms, such as claiming that a competitor lacks the experience necessary to service the machines which he sells or that a competitor has gone out of business or discontinued sales of his products when he has not. It must not be forgotten, however, that the truth is still the ultimate measure of what is unfair. A commission order prohibiting disparagement of a competitor's financial standing was reversed, on the grounds that "it was true, and we know of no standard of practice which forbids the telling of the truth, even about a competitor."[13]

A competitor with a little-known name may try to pass off his goods as those manufactured by a firm with a well-known name. Close similarities between names sometimes will accomplish the desired result. Or the fact that one part of a total product was manufactured by a well-known corporation will be distorted to the point where the consumer thinks the total product is manufactured by the "big-name" company.

[13] *Philip Carey Mfg. Co. v. Federal Trade Commission,* 29 F.2d 49, 52 (1928).

## BAIT ADVERTISING

The Commission has found it necessary to issue guides against bait advertising. The basic idea inherent in such advertising is to present an alluring offer to the consumer which does not represent a bona fide effort to sell the advertised product. It is a "switch scheme" involving a bait, such as a spectacularly low price, to lure the unwary buyer toward another, usually higher-priced, good. Among the specific acts condemned in the Commission's guides against bait advertising are the refusal to show or sell the product, disparagement by acts or words of the advertised product or the terms of sale or availability or serviceability of it, the failure to have the product available in reasonable quantities, the refusal to take orders to be delivered within a reasonable period of time, the showing of a product which is defective or impractical, and the use of a salesman's compensation plan which discourages the salesmen from trying to sell the advertised product. According to the Commission's view, actual sale of the advertised product does not preclude the existence of a switch scheme, for it has been found that actual sale of the advertised product is sometimes only the beginning of the scheme.

## DECEPTIVE PRICING PRACTICES

Deceptive pricing practices have taken several different forms. As a result, the Federal Trade Commission has issued several guides in this area of possible misrepresentation. Making price comparisons which are not entirely valid has been a serious abuse in the advertising of prices. The Commission requires that savings claims must relate, to the best of the seller's ability, to the real market prices. Artificial markups and comparisons with past prices which are not normal are not permitted. Where price comparisons are made with comparable and similar merchandise, such comparable merchandise must be of like grade and quality in all material respects and generally available in the same market.

A price practice which has been the subject of abuse is "pre-ticketing," by which the manufacturer affixes to the article a tag or label showing the retail price. To draw a line through the printed price and mark a new lower price, or simply to advertise actual sales price at a lower figure, gives the retailer the opportunity to present the impression of a special price reduction. Preticketing may be an old custom in some lines of goods, but it nevertheless provides the manufacturer as well as the retailer an opportunity to utilize this device as a means to promote "bargain" sales of the manufacturer's goods. Thus the manufacturer who pretickets or who makes use of suggested price lists must have a good idea of actual retail prices or make an honest estimate thereof if he is to remain free of a deceptive-pricing charge. The Commission holds the manufacturer responsible, although the act of preticketing is not illegal per se.[14]

The more volatile the retail prices, the more difficult it is for the manufacturer to comply with the law against preticketing as a deceptive-pricing device. If, on the other hand, retailers of the good in a given market are all charging the same rigid price, then there is the suggestion that pricing may be illegal under the laws against restraint of trade.[15] The use of "suggested price" lists by manufacturers involves the same hazard.

It is interesting to note that the Automobile Information Disclosure Act of 1958 *requires* that automobile manufacturers preticket new automobiles. A purpose of the act was to prevent deceptive pricing by eliminating "price-packing," a practice by dealers of marking up or adding charges over and above the normal recognized markup to offset overallowances on the trade-in value of the customer's used car. Whereas at one time this practice had enabled buyers to use their almost worthless old-car trade-in to meet down-payment requirements, it could also be used by the dealers as a means of obtaining higher profits. Unless the retail customer had a clear idea of what the normal retail prices were, he could be given a large trade-in value which was, unknown to the buyer, accompanied by a large price pack. Valid price comparisons by the consumer were, therefore, somewhat difficult to make. The Department of Justice opposed the passage of this legislation, arguing that the preticketing requirements of the act gave the manufacturer a tool to facilitate resale

---

[14] *Baltimore Luggage Co. v. Federal Trade Commission,* 296 F.2d 608, 610 (1961), *cert. denied,* 369 U.S. 860 (1962).

[15] *Rayex Corp. et al.,* Federal Trade Commission Docket 7346 (1962).

price maintenance. For this reason it argued instead for pre-ticketing which would indicate the price to the dealer.

Another practice involving misrepresentation is the use of the word "free." Prior to 1953 the Federal Trade Commission forbade the use of the word if it was conditioned upon the purchase of other merchandise or the performance of a service. In that year, however, the Commission adopted a general rule which allows use of this word even if there is a condition attached, but requires that the prerequisites to receiving the "free" good be "clearly and conspicuously set forth at the outset so as to leave no reasonable probability that the terms of the offer will be misunderstood."[16] This means, specifically, that the conditions or attached obligations must appear in close conjunction with the word "free" (or words of similar meaning) when that word first appears in the offer. A footnote reference made by use of an asterisk or other symbol is not adequate. Furthermore, this presentation is not sufficient if the quality of the "tying" product is lowered, its ordinary and usual price raised, or its quantity or size reduced. This is the wording and requirement of the Commission's "free goods" rule which appears in standard form in the trade practice rules for industries where such a rule is relevant.

## THE TEXTILE AND FUR LABELING LAWS

The wearing-apparel industry has been singled out for special legislation because of widespread abuses with respect to the description of products. Consumer ignorance of the fiber content of textile fabrics and the true nature of furs and fur products made misrepresentation relatively easy and the maintenance of honest competition difficult. The honest competitor could lose out to the dishonest competitor. And the consumer, of course, was an ultimate loser.

The Federal Trade Commission has been given jurisdiction over three acts relating to the labeling of products of this industry, with authority to draw up implementing rules and regulations. The Wool Products Labeling Act of 1939 was aimed at the

---

[16] The new rule conforms to the opinion of the Commission dismissing the complaint in *Walter J. Black, Inc.,* 50 F.T.C. 225 (1953). Commissioner Mead, dissenting, said, "This is a case about 'free' books which were not free" (at 236).

misbranding of wool products, and requires that wool products give by stamp, tag, or label their percentage of wool and other fibers and the name of the manufacturer or distributor. The Fur Products Labeling Act of 1951 requires that fur content of fur products be properly identified in all respects. The Textile Fiber Products Identification Act of 1958 applies to textile fiber products which are in final form for marketing to the consumer. It requires identification of the different textile fibers by percentage content, the name of the manufacturer or distributor, and the country of origin if imported. Disclosure of similar information, except for percentage breakdown, must also be made in advertisements of these products.

Prior to these special acts of legislation the Federal Trade Commission had proceeded against the abuses present in these areas under Section 5's prohibition of unfair methods of competition and unfair and deceptive acts or practices. The practices cited in these three acts are specifically designated as unfair and deceptive acts or practices under the Federal Trade Commission Act. But the Commission's authority to make rules and regulations to help implement the administration and enforcement of these laws eliminates the uncertainties that might be inherent in the general language of Section 5. For wool products, the Commission has provided rules about exactly what information, and in what order, must appear on the stamps, tags, or labels. For furs and fur products, a fur-products name guide has been provided to the members of the industry. Such names are the only ones which can be used in the labeling of fur products and in the advertising and invoicing of fur products and furs. For textile fiber products, the Commission has officially assigned generic names to the new synthetic fibers. In short, the law has been reduced to specifics.

Under the wool law false or deceptive labeling or failure to carry a label is considered misbranding. In addition to being handled or remedied under the same procedures as any other unfair and deceptive practice under the Federal Trade Commission Act, the goods believed to be violating the law are subject to condemnation and confiscation through district court proceedings, and the Commission can seek an injunction pending final outcome of its usual procedures. A person wilfully violating the act may be fined up to $5,000 and/or imprisoned for not more than one year. The fur and textile product labeling laws are somewhat broader in their scope than the wool act. In addition to requiring information that must be on the labels, they cover false advertising and invoicing. The textile fiber labeling law does not, however, provide for condemnation proceedings.

## FOODS

The principles which apply to the Federal Trade Commission's attack on misrepresentations in general apply also to food. Section 12 of the Federal Trade Commission Act specifically refers to the false advertisement of food and declares it to be "an unfair or deceptive act or practice in commerce within the meaning of section 5." With respect to food, however, the Commission has the power to seek an injunction which remains in force while the Commission processes its complaint. And Section 15 is fairly specific, stating that in determining illegal, misleading advertisements "representations made or suggested by statement, word, design, device, sound, or any combination thereof" should be taken into account. The extent to which an advertisement fails to reveal material facts, especially with respect to consequences of use, is also to be considered.

We shall confine ourselves in this section largely to the work of the Food and Drug Administration which, under the Federal Food, Drug, and Cosmetic Act, attacks the "misbranding" of foods. The Food and Drug Administration administers the act with the assistance of regulations which the act has authorized it to promulgate. The act provides for possible use of the injunction, penalties of fines or imprisonment, and seizure of goods.

The Food, Drug, and Cosmetic Act considers a food as misbranded if the labeling is false or misleading in any particular, if it is offered for sale under the name of another food, if it is an imitation of another food, if its container is so "made, formed, or fitted" as to be misleading, and if the package does not indicate both the name and place of business of the manufacturer, packer, or distributor, and if in package form, statements of the quantity of the contents in terms of weight, measure, or numerical count are not accurate. Where the food in question is one which purports to be one for which the Food and Drug Administration has established standards of identity and quality, it must conform to those standards, and the label must bear the name of the food as specified in the Food and Drug Administration's regulations and, where required, the common names of optional ingredients present (other than spices, flavoring, and coloring). Standards of fill of the container may also be prescribed. Where prescribed standards of quality or fill are not met, information to this effect must be carried on the label. Required information must be prominently placed on the label and in such terms that it will likely be read and understood by the ordinary consumer. Where standards of identity have not been established, the label must show the common or usual name of the food and ingredients except that spices, flavorings, and colorings may simply be designated as such. Where foods are represented as being for special dietary uses, the label must carry the prescribed information, and where artificial flavors or colorings or chemical preservatives are used, the labels must clearly indicate those facts. Where pesticide chemicals have been applied to raw agricultural commodities, before they have been removed from the shipping container for resale, this fact, including the name and the function of the chemical, must be shown. In other words, these labeling requirements are not only negative, declaring against labeling which is false and misleading, but also positive, requiring full information about contents on the label. The labeling requirements are indeed comprehensive, providing exemption only where small packages or impracticalities of the regulations might exist.

Under the requirements for labeling for foods, bonitos, for example, cannot be offered for sale as tuna. The phrase "kosher style" cannot be used on products that do not meet religious dietary requirements. Fish cannot be sold as "Cape Cod fillet" unless it comes from that region. The use of trade names implying that substantial amounts of egg or milk are in food products when the true content does not justify such a reference is false and misleading. A canner of fresh fruits and vegetables can use the terms "Grade A," "Grade B," and "Grade C," but if he does so he must conform to these grades as defined by the United States Department of Agriculture—he cannot use his own grading system. Saccharin tablets, when sold to the consumer as a sweetening agent, must bear labels stating that the tablets have no food value. Artificially sweetened jam or jelly must be labeled as an imitation. Representations that salad oils, shortenings, oleomargarine, or similar products containing unsaturated fats and oils would help to prevent heart attacks and reduce blood cholesterol are considered false and misleading.

Misleading containers are not permissible; but to establish clear standards in this matter is indeed difficult, for different products may carry their own special packaging requirements and problems. Some products require a certain amount of empty space inside the cardboard container, such as cake frosting which is in tubes with clipped ends. Some materials, such as cocoa, settle after packing. The desire to utilize packages of artistic design may require empty packaging space. Certainly, all slack-filled or large-size packages do not represent deliberate efforts to mislead or defraud. The packager, however, must guard against excessive avoidable space in the package. The problem is not limited to slack-filled packages. Wrapping partially smoked fish in orange transparent cellophane gives the fish the appearance of being fully smoked. The molding of half-shapes of novelty candy and then nesting them in shredded cellophane gives the appearance of full shapes or candy double the true size. In both these cases, the consumer may be misled.

Weight, measure, and numerical count with respect to the quantity in a package have been sources of confusion to the average consumer. The same product may be sold in 13½-, 15¼-, and 17½-ounce packages. In one product line packages were selling in sixty-nine different weights, all under three pounds.[17] What do "small," "medium," "large," and "super" really represent? Is the "economy size" really the lowest-cost-per-ounce size? What is a "jumbo quart"?—is it any different from a "full quart," or even the "quart"? How many ounces or pounds are involved in "four servings"? Meeting the problem of resolving such confusions for the consumer is a difficult task for the Food and Drug Administration.

Colored margarine (or oleomargarine) is singled out for special attention by the law. This food product is such a close sub-

---

[17] 108 Cong. Rec. 19,266 (1962).

stitute for butter in terms of appearance and taste that the consumer may be easily deceived. This fact, coupled with pressure from the dairy interests, has led to the passage of several pieces of legislation which have the effect of restricting the sale of margarine. Section 15 of the Federal Trade Commission Act provides specifically that a margarine advertisement shall be deemed misleading in a material respect if representations are made or suggested that the oleomargarine is a dairy product. Thus to describe oleomargarine as "creamy smooth" or "churned fresh daily" is enough to condemn such advertisements as being unlawful.

Colored margarine is also singled out for special attention in the Federal Food, Drug, and Cosmetic Act. No person may sell colored margarine at retail unless it is sold in packages of one pound or less of net weight and there appears on the label the word "oleomargarine" or "margarine" in type or lettering at least as large as any other type of lettering on the label. There must also appear on the label of the package a full and accurate statement of all the ingredients, and each part of the contents of the package must be in a wrapper which bears the word "oleomargarine" or "margarine" in type or lettering not smaller than 20-point type. Furthermore, colored margarine cannot be served at public eating places unless signs are conspicuously posted to this effect or it is clearly stated on the menu, and each separate serving of margarine must be either clearly labeled or served in a triangular shape.

Most of the states have laws regulating the sale of colored margarine, and many of these are similar to the Federal Food, Drug, and Cosmetic Act. Some states have placed further direct or indirect restrictions on the sale of yellow margarine. Wisconsin still prohibits the manufacture or sale of this product. Pennsylvania prohibits its serving in public eating places. And several states impose heavy taxes on the product.

## DRUGS, DEVICES, AND COSMETICS

The Federal Trade Commission has specific authority, as with food, to regulate the false advertisements of drugs, therapeutic devices, and cosmetics under Sections 12 to 15 of the Federal Trade Commission Act, and may seek an injunction. The Commission has issued orders against representations made in support of dentifrices, face creams, hair preparations, hair destroyers, hair-growth preparations,[18] "medicated" soaps, vitamins in cosmetics, diathermy and electrolytic devices, eyeglasses and sunglasses, hearing aids, and various would-be health foods. Attacks on remedies for alcoholism, colds, diabetes, ills of the kidney and liver, and rheumatism and arthritis have consumed a considerable amount of the Commission's time. With respect to these products, an advertisement which is misleading in a material respect includes not only misrepresentations made or suggested in any way but also failure to reveal material facts. It is not necessary to show a fraudulent intent.

The Federal Food, Drug, and Cosmetic Act controls the labeling and packaging of drugs, devices, and cosmetics. Although spelled out in separate sections of the act, these controls are essentially the same as the controls over food. Misbranding provisions for drugs and devices are more extensive, largely because they require more complete identification of the products, such as the ingredients, the common or established (standard or official) name of the drug as well as the brand name, directions for use, and possible harmful effects. A tightening of the Food, Drug, and Cosmetic Act was represented by a 1962 amendment which states that a new drug may not be approved for marketing if it is found that the proposed labeling is false or misleading in any particular, whether in relation to the drug's claimed effect or otherwise. Labeling of drugs must also keep current with new evidence which may be discovered with respect to the drug; otherwise the drug may be ordered withdrawn from the market.

With respect to prescription drugs, 1962 amendments to the Food, Drug, and Cosmetic Act brought the jurisdiction of the Food and Drug Administration directly into the field of advertising control. Prescription drug advertisements must show the established name in type at least half as large as that used for the brand name (a requirement also true of the labeling of prescription drugs), the drug's quantitative formula, and a true and

---

[18] The courts have upheld the Commission on the view that there is no known scientific means of preventing or overcoming baldness. *David W. Erickson v. Federal Trade Commission,* 272 F.2d 318 (1959); *George M. Voss v. Federal Trade Commission,* 275 F.2d 24 (1960).

nonmisleading brief summary of adverse side effects, contraindications (any condition of disease which makes the medication inadvisable), and effectiveness of the drug. These advertisements may not be disseminated without the prior approval of the Food and Drug Administration unless the sponsor of the prescription drug develops a satisfactory program of advertising to publicize information on side effects or contraindications involving fatalities or serious injury.

## HAZARDOUS SUBSTANCES

The Food and Drug Administration was singled out to administer the Federal Hazardous Substances Labeling Act of 1960. This law was passed to ensure that proper labels were affixed to toxic, corrosive, or irritating or flammable goods which tend to enter into ordinary household use. It supplemented, with its much more rigorous requirements, Federal Trade Commission actions under Section 5 of the Federal Trade Commission Act. Labels must state conspicuously the name and place of business of the manufacturer, packer, distributor, or seller; the name of the hazardous substance; the words "Danger," "Warning," or "Caution" where applicable; an affirmative statement of the principal hazard, e.g., "absorbed through the skin"; precautionary measures to be followed and instructions, where appropriate, for first aid; any special handling or storage instructions; and the statement, "Keep out of the Reach of Children," or its practical equivalent. This act permits use of court injunctions, and the courts may issue decrees of condemnation. In its first year of enforcement of this act the Food and Drug Administration seized more than a dozen types of hazardous household products in twenty-five separate actions on charges that labeling was inadequate to warn users of their potential danger.[19]

## YESTERDAY AND TODAY

In the last fifty-odd years the growing body of statutes and rules covering false advertising and labeling has indicated a decreasing tolerance of society toward the efforts of sellers of goods and serv-

---

[19] Feb. 1, 1962 to Feb. 1, 1963. *FDA Report on Enforcement and Compliance,* 1963, p. 6.

ices to take advantage of consumer ignorance and gullibility. The practices which existed before the passage of the first Federal legislation in this field were often quite flagrant. Additions to this body of legislation have been made over the years as the need for more complete surveillance over false advertising, misbranding, and inadequate labeling has been thought necessary. Such new legislation has sometimes been brought into being directly upon the heels of some major incident in which unprotected consumers met with death or injury.

Today misrepresentations of products are not legally acceptable. Foods, drugs, therapeutic devices, cosmetics, textiles, furs, and hazardous substances must meet certain labeling standards. But deception of the consumer continues to persist to some degree. Some deceptions are unintended, the result of enthusiastic exaggeration. Other deceptions derive simply from the profit known to result from this form of competition for the consumer's dollar. In short, the problems of deceptive advertising and misrepresentation are not entirely eliminated.

Today's economic citizen may be more sophisticated in many ways than yesterday's. And he has been aided greatly in making more intelligent decisions in the marketplace by government requirements with respect to advertising and labeling. There is no reason, however, to believe that he is less gullible. For he is still credulous, and still looking for bargains and cure-alls.

## SUGGESTIONS FOR FURTHER READING

Several books were published in the late 1920s and early 1930s which helped toward the passage in 1938 of legislation which provided tighter legal controls over advertising and selling, especially of foods, drugs, and cosmetics: Stuart Chase and F. J. Schlink, *Your Money's Worth,* The Macmillan Co., New York, 1927; Arthur Kallet and F. J. Schlink, *100,000,000 Guinea Pigs,* Vanguard Press, Inc., New York, 1932; Arthur Kallett, *Counterfeit,* Vanguard Press, Inc., New York, 1935; F. J. Schlink, *Eat, Drink and Be Wary,* Covici, Friede, Inc., New York, 1935; and Ruth deForest Lamb, *American Chamber of Horrors,* Holt, Rinehart and Winston, Inc., New York, 1936.

The story of the passage of food, drugs, and cosmetics legislation is told in Stephen Wilson, *Food & Drug Regulation,* American Council on Public Affairs, Washington, 1942. Some sixty-five short articles by different authorities on various phases of food, drug, and cosmetic regulation are in Henry Welch and Marti-Ibañez, *The Impact of the Food and Drug Administration on Our Society,* MD Publications, Inc., New York, 1956. Current developments can be followed in the Commerce Clearing House, *Food, Drug, and Cosmetic Law Reporter,* and in the Annual Reports of the Department of Health, Education, and Welfare.

Testimony and exhibits in *Hearings before the Subcommittee on Antitrust and Monopoly of the Senate Committee on the Judiciary* have as their subject *Packaging and Labeling Practices,* 87th Cong., 1st Sess., 1961, parts 1 and 2, and *Packaging and Labeling Legislation,* 88th Cong., 1st Sess., 1963. *Automobile Price Labeling* is the subject of *Hearings before the Automobile Marketing Subcommittee of the Senate Committee on Interstate and Foreign Commerce,* 85th Cong., 2d Sess., 1958. *False and Misleading Advertising* is the subject of *Hearings before the Subcommittee of the House Committee on Government Operations,* 85th Cong., 2d Sess., 1958, and House Reports of this Committee are concerned with the advertising of filter-tip cigarettes (1372), weight-reducing remedies (2553), dentifrices (2667), and prescription tranquilizing drugs (2668). Current activities of the Federal Trade Commission with respect to misrepresentation can be followed in the Commission's *Advertising Alert* (monthly).

*Advertising Age* for Jan. 15, 1963, pp. 166–198, provides a general survey of the regulation of advertising both by governmental units and by self-policing.

# 6

# *UNFAIR*
# *TRADE PRACTICES*

Competition is not free of methods which are considered unethical. Business practices sometimes fall short of measuring up to the levels of morality considered desirable by the majority. Fraudulent selling with its deliberate intent to deceive, although practiced by a limited few, is the worst of such practices.

Codes of ethics are not available for business as they are for the professions such as medicine or the law. This lack can be partly accounted for by the fact that a personal relationship such as that between a practitioner and his client does not usually exist between the seller and buyer of goods. Furthermore, the large numbers present in the distributive trades work to prevent the group itself from enforcing high standards of business conduct. For these reasons the law must assist in protecting both the honest tradesman and the consumer from the unscrupulous competitor.

In this chapter we shall examine the principal regulatory authorities which pertain to unfair trade practices and the nature of the practices which must be controlled. Unfair or fraudulent competitive practices are manifold. Our approach is one of describing certain basic practices and presenting legal principles. To attempt to quantify by anything more than a suggestion would result only in inaccuracy. In most cases only a fringe of the business community is guilty of unfair practices, but the danger exists that, unless the unfair trade practices are brought under control, a large part of the business community will be forced to adopt these practices in order to stay in the competition.

## AUTHORITIES FOR REGULATION OF UNFAIR TRADE PRACTICES

Trade practice conference rules can be established on an industry-by-industry basis with the help of the Federal Trade Commission in an attempt to prevent the use of unfair methods of competition. But there are almost always a few recalcitrants who find it profitable to stray from the accepted standards of business conduct; thus the significance of Section 5 of the Federal Trade Commission Act prohibiting unfair methods of competition and unfair or deceptive acts or practices in interstate commerce. The Commission, with its cease and desist orders, is a necessary watchdog. Its arm, however, can reach only into interstate commerce. Actually, it is more than a watchdog. It is an agency which helps to define, by its enforcement actions, what is fair and what is unfair. It can, by establishing legal standards, also help to establish ethical standards.

The Post Office Department can help to prevent fraudulent selling. The mails cannot be used to defraud. A problem, of course, is detecting which mail is the offending mail.

Some of the misleading sales tactics and fraudulent selling occur in local communities, sometimes in door-to-door selling. It is necessary, therefore, in combatting unfair selling practices to have state and local laws. State and local laws against unfair and fraudulent selling are likely to be closely related to laws against false advertising, for sales which are unfair or fraudulent frequently, if not usually, result from the deception or misrepresentation of advertising. Better Business Bureaus, where they exist, can provide an important assist in this area. Most of the states have laws making it a criminal offense to collect money under false pretenses. Control of weights and measures to eliminate deception in selling is a significant item in local regulation.

Some communities try to control door-to-door selling by requiring peddlers to obtain a license, which will be granted only after the applicant's character has been checked. Some communities have so-called "Green River" ordinances, which forbid salesmen from going in and upon private residences for the purpose of soliciting orders for goods without the prior consent of the occupant. Although principally designed to protect local tradesmen from the competition of transient sellers, they have the effect of limiting the opportunities of traveling gyps.

The consumer who has been swindled can turn to the courts and attempt to recover his losses under the common law. Here the consumer can seek private damages, but procedure is slow and costly and often without satisfactory results. The swindler may have absconded with a down payment, never to be heard from again. Or the seller may even have the law technically on his side. To demonstrate a deliberate intent to deceive may prove difficult.

### UNFAIR AND FRAUDULENT LOCAL SELLING

Mrs. Housewife may have little or no intention of doing business with door-to-door salesmen, but she may still become victim of a selling racket. Admittance to a home may be obtained by the caller's announcing, "You have won a contest." Or the caller may represent himself as an interviewer for a marketing research firm. Or the salesman may represent an encyclopedia firm which claims that it wishes to obtain the right to use the householder's endorsement. The entrée is then followed up by an intensive selling effort, as a result of which the housewife may commit herself to a purchase which brings with it some additional "free" good or is at a price which is supposed to represent a big "discount"; but in reality the price is the same as that to any other buyer.

The consumer himself may have found it necessary to call in or go to a specialist dealing in home appliances or equipment. Radio and television repair has been a ripe field for the practice of fraud. How is the average consumer to know whether all the repairs and replacements being made are truly necessary? Garage mechanics may claim to find "badly worn" parts in addition to those for which the car was originally brought into the garage for replacement. The more technical modern appliances and equipment become, the more vulnerable the consumer is to the fraudulent repairman.

The advance-fee racket can be costly to the unwary. A person claiming to represent a real estate agency with listings on a national basis and an extremely good sales record will call on the homeowner who wishes to sell his property. Collecting part of the fee in advance, the "agent" will never be heard from again. Another version is that of the salesman who has a buyer sign a contract where some entries are still to be filled in. As a result, the final price for the good in question turns out to be higher than the buyer had thought. In this case the seller has not disappeared with his fee; rather the seller, or perhaps a finance company, now holds a binding contract.

Other means of deceptive selling at the local level could be cited. Medical quackery is probably one of the most fruitful fields for deception as desperate people seek cures for as yet incurable diseases. Fake devices which are claimed to measure electrical frequencies emanating from the body as a means of diagnosis are used on the uninformed. Charlatans practice marriage counseling and psychiatry. And "hair experts" give treatments guaranteed to save or restore hair.

## INFLUENCING SALES BY UNFAIR PRODUCT POLICIES

Shipping goods which have not been ordered to business customers is a sales practice against which the Federal Trade Commission has issued cease and desist orders. This practice can assume various guises. Purchasers' orders can be padded by preparing order blanks in such a way that the buyer is misled about the actual quantity he is committing himself to pay for. Another method is for a seller to ship goods which have never been ordered. Perhaps the seller simply sends a larger quantity than had been ordered. Or maybe the customer had asked for and received "free samples" and then the seller had followed this up with billing the customer for those goods. A less harmful, but nonetheless unfair, related tactic is to ship unordered merchandise to a distribution outlet with the hope that the distributor, having once seen the goods, can be induced to buy them. Perhaps a special added inducement will then be provided by offering to extend credit terms or to assist in the reselling of such goods.

Another version of this selling technique is to substitute other, perhaps inferior-quality, goods for those ordered when shipment is made. Federal Trade Commission orders in this category have usually involved delivery of inferior goods: books with paper or bindings cheaper than those of books advertised or shown by salesmen, glass or ceramic rather than aluminum cooking utensils, hosiery of lower quality or different colors than that ordered, unbranded goods rather than trademarked goods, rusted or corroded pipes rather than clean ones, and shirts having design or style different from that of those ordered. In any case, equivalence of substituted goods is no defense.[1]

The practice of shipping unordered goods has another side: this is the failure to ship ordered goods, or shipping later than promised or only after unreasonable delays. This market behavior is unfair to the user and has been condemned by the Federal Trade Commission. If the timing of delivery is crucial to the user of the merchandise, the practice can be disruptive to the customer's use or production plans. Where the goods are paid for in advance, the customer's funds held by the seller amount to an interest-free loan to the seller. This practice can result from a seller's willingness to take orders for more business than he knows he can handle in an effort to preempt the sales of competitors, from pure negligence, or from disregard of customers' rights once payment has been received.

## INFLUENCING BUYERS' EMPLOYEES

The vigor of competition may be such that the manufacturer or distributor of a good may find it profitable to encourage sales by financially rewarding the individual salesmen of their commercial customers who consummate the sales made to the next buyer. The financial reward to the employee for pushing a particular manufacturer's product is known as "push money."

Originally the Federal Trade Commission took the position that push-money arrangements were a clear violation of Section 5, for it saw the competing products suffering a corresponding competitive disadvantage. Thus it prohibited the arrangement whether the salesman's employer had consented to it or not. But a court decision in 1921 held that the practice was not illegal

---

[1] *Federal Trade Commission v. Algoma Lumber Co.*, 291 U.S. 67, 76–77 (1934).

if it was done with the consent of the employer.[2] The reasoning of the court in this case, wherein the manufacturer was giving premiums such as necktie sets to the salesmen of merchants handling his goods (bedsprings and kindred products), was that the manufacturer had sold the goods to the merchant, and thus, as far as he was concerned, his interest in the goods had ended. The competition among the manufacturers had ceased, said the court, and thus the manufacturer could not be attacked for engaging in unfair competition. Furthermore, said the court, a merchant, or his salesmen with his consent, has the right to discriminate between the goods he has to sell. Nor does he have to tell his customers about whatever particular incentives he may have to sell certain goods. To be more specific, the court said that it could see no evidence of fraud. As for any possible misrepresentation, such deception, if present, would have been illegal on its own basis; but none was present in the eyes of the court in this case.

This holding by the court that a manufacturer's interest in the competition ends as soon as the goods have been sold by that manufacturer represents somewhat unrealistic thinking. The Commission since then has, however, limited its attacks to that push money which is offered without the full knowledge of the salesman's employer. The practice has been sufficiently prevalent that push-money rules have appeared in the trade practice rules of several industries. A standardized rule adopted in 1953 was revised in 1962. Under the terms of this standard rule, the granting of anything of value to a salesperson employed by a customer as an inducement for special sales effort is illegal where the payments are made without the knowledge and consent of the salesperson's employer, where the payment is dependent on a lottery scheme, where the terms of the inducement would unduly hamper the sale of the competitive products or substantially lessen competition or tend to create a monopoly, or where the manufacturer does not make the same inducements available on proportionally equal terms to salespersons of competing customers. If push-money payments are transferred by the salesperson to his employer, or if they result in a corresponding re-

---

[2] *Kinney-Rome Co. v. Federal Trade Commission,* 275 Fed. 665 (1921).

duction in the salesperson's salary, then they would not be considered an unfair method of competition under the rule, but would be considered under the price discrimination provisions of the Robinson-Patman Act.

Commercial bribery is much like the practice of giving push money. But the payments to the customer's employee are made to induce purchases from the party who is making the payments. These payments are made secretly. In other words, such payments are made to employees of customers, of prospective customers, or of competitors' customers without the knowledge or consent of their employers. The practice has been found by the Federal Trade Commission to be an unfair method of competition. Commercial bribery is also specifically denounced in the Federal Alcohol Administration Act with respect to the sale of distilled spirits, wine, or malt beverages.

A court decision in 1920 seemed to place limits on the ability of the Federal Trade Commission to attack this practice, and the number of successfully processed complaints against commercial bribery has been small. Reversing an order of the Commission, a court of appeals held that gratuities such as liquor, cigars, meals, theater tickets, entertainment, and the like granted to employees of customers were not unlawful, for "the method of entertainment found to be unfair has been an incident of business from time immemorial."[3] Even the payment of money itself was seen by this court to be, rather, a matter of fraud to be settled between the purchasing company and the supplier, for the bribe monies presumably were included in the purchase price of the goods and the merchant could thus recover the overcharge in a private suit. The Commission, nevertheless, has issued cease and desist orders, which have not been appealed, in a few commercial bribery cases since that decision. And in these decisions the Commission has found the giving of cigars, meals, and entertainment as well as substantial sums of money to be unfair methods of competition.

In 1960 the Commission actively and successfully (through some eighty consent orders) prohibited *payola* payments by rec-

---

[3] *New Jersey Asbestos Co. v. Federal Trade Commission*, 264 Fed. 509, 510–511 (1920).

ord manufacturers and distributors to the personnel of broad-casting stations, especially disc jockeys, to push the sales of certain records. The Commission held that the resulting promo-tion of particular records on radio and television led the public to believe that these records were the most popular and that this in turn caused the records to be more popular, resulting in sub-stantial increases in sales. To remove the element of deception the Commission requires that if any payments to any broad-casting station personnel are made, whether direct or indirect, and whether the personnel are employee or employer, these facts must be disclosed to the listening public. Such disclosure pre-sumably will cause the listener to be more objective in arriving at his own decision about whether he wants to buy a certain record. But in any case, even though payola is now barred under Section 5 unless fully conceded to the listening public, it is be-lieved by some that the subtle pressures on favored customers by record manufacturers can cause ratings of best-seller records to be manipulated.[4]

### INTERFERENCE WITH COMPETITORS

Interference with selling efforts of competitors can actually take the form of physical interference. It is not at all surprising that the Federal Trade Commission should condemn such tactics as unfair methods of competition. What is surprising is that such practices have existed at all. Tampering with competitors' demonstrators and causing poor demonstrator performance, diluting a competitor's liquid products to lessen quality, dis-mantling equipment and misrepresenting the condition of equip-ment (such as a household furnace) of a competitor, or obliterat-ing the manufacturer's name on a product when servicing that competitor's product are examples of these unfair practices.

Most forms of interference with competitors' selling efforts are not quite so gross as those described above but may be equally damaging, and the Federal Trade Commission has suc-cesfully attacked various forms of this practice. Attaching false shipping instructions to competitors' packages can cause much

[4] Robert E. Dallas, "Some in Record Field Say 'Pressures' Make Hit Tune Lists Invalid," *The Wall Street Journal,* May 17, 1963, pp. 1, 14.

trouble. Buying up competitors' mail-order catalogs or systematically causing such catalogs to be requested by bogus customers can add to the mail-order house's costs and deprive its customers of their sources for orders. Buying up competitors' samples has a similar unfair effect. Buying up competitors' inventory stocks in times of shortage can contribute to the denial of customer acceptance of the competitor and his products.

Sending fictitious requests for estimates, specifications, and prices to competitors through the mails on a large scale can be irritating, time-consuming, and costly to the competitors. Arranging with retailers to remove competitors' products from mounts bearing trademarks and remounting them on blank ones or placing them in a display where only the rearranger's trade name is showing are interferences with trademark identification. Instituting, or the instigating or financing of others to institute, lawsuits which are designed merely to annoy the competitor is an unfair method of competition.

The threat or the actual filing of a patent infringement suit can be an unfair method of competition where bad faith is found to be present. Such sham actions can be used to intimidate competitors or customers of competitors. But threats or actual filings of patent infringement suits are to be found in the legitimate course of business affairs, and at law good faith is assumed until proven otherwise.

Unfair interference with a competitor can be accomplished by inducing or attempting to induce the competitor's customers or suppliers to breach their contract with him. Any such efforts, including furnishing the prospective customer with legal services or helping him to compose letters which would seek to evade the contract responsibilities, are unfair. It is more typical of this unfair method of competition simply to malign the competitor in order to induce a shift in business.

One direct way which has been used to injure a competitor, and at the same time help one's self in a positive way, is to induce key employees of a competitor to leave their employer to work for their employer's competitor. Cease and desist orders covering this practice have been but a handful, presumably because labor mobility and the right of labor to seek out maximum wages and salaries are concepts dear to the American's heart. But some instances of this pirating of labor have clearly had an unfair competitive intent. For example, the truck drivers who collected fats, bones, suet, and hides for companies who rendered or processed such substances were enticed away through higher wages by a competitor who wished to learn of and take over these sources of supply.[5]

The stealing of competitors' trade secrets is an unfair method of competition. Employees may resign and take up new employment, carrying with them data on production methods, lists of customers, plans for contract bids, and new products. Employees of a firm can be paid for transmitting confidential information. Or a firm can use spies or detectives to ferret out information on competitors. To prove successfully theft of a trade secret is difficult, for it is an idea or piece of knowledge rather than a product. It is necessary to demonstrate that the information stolen had value, was a secret and not known to other persons in that area of knowledge, and was not developed by the alleged thief himself on his own time.

The unfair acquisition or threatened acquisition of trade secrets can be handled at law by four basic methods, depending partly on the facts in the case. It can be considered a theft, the alleged thief being prosecuted by a district attorney for a felony, embezzlement, or illegal use of the mails. Second, an employer can sue an employee or former employee for damages resulting from the disclosure to others of trade secrets. Third, an employer can seek a court injunction that restrains a former employee from disclosing trade secrets to his new employer.[6] Finally, the Federal Trade Commission can issue a cease and desist order. The Commission's activity in this area was confined to its early years. But it has issued orders in cases involving spying on competitors, placing detectives in competitors' plants, obtaining information on competitors' shipments from railroad employees and similar espionage to obtain the identity of competitors' customers, and paying a competitor's employees or former employees for confidential information about the competitor.

---

[5] *Darling & Company*, 30 F.T.C. 739 (1940).
[6] See "Legal Hurdle for Job-hoppers," *Business Week*, June 1, 1963, pp. 95–96.

## LOTTERY DEVICES

The use of lottery devices to assist in selling goods is a clear violation of Section 5 as an unfair method of competition. In the words of a court of appeals in 1958: "The law is now firmly established that the practice of selling goods by means which involve a game of chance, gift enterprise or lottery, including push cards . . . is contrary to the established public policy of the United States."[7] The Federal Trade Commission first condemned the practice in 1925. The Supreme Court first ruled on the issue nine years later, holding that the particular practice involved in the case, the sale of penny candies, exploited children. Furthermore, said the court, although lotteries were not deceptive, such devices had been condemned by the community and had long been held contrary to public policy by common law and criminal statutes, and those competitors who thus held out against using the device suffered a loss of business. In short, "it would seem a gross perversion of the normal meaning of the word, which is the first criterion of statutory construction, to hold that the method is not 'unfair.' "[8] Although the use of lottery devices has been most prevalent in the candy and novelty-merchandise industries, the legal prohibition applies to the marketing of all goods. The law on this point is well-established, the Commission issuing a very large number of orders and the courts, on appeals, almost always affirming these orders.

The strength of the legal attitude against the use of lottery devices to market goods is also evidenced by the existence of state and local statutes against the practice. Post Office Department regulations represent this general attitude by stating that any letter, package, postal card, or circular with respect to any lottery or gift enterprise and lottery tickets are nonmailable matter.

Lottery devices are to be condemned under Section 5 when two conditions are present. First, interstate commerce must be involved. In the only other ruling that the Supreme Court has made on lotteries, it held that the strictly intrastate manufacture

[7] *Surf Sales Co. v. Federal Trade Commission*, 259 F.2d 744, 746 (1958).
[8] *Federal Trade Commission v. R. F. Keppel and Bro., Inc.*, 291 U.S. 304, 313 (1934).

and sale (of candy) by the lottery method could not be reached under this statute.[9] However, a lottery device can be condemned merely because it is sold or distributed, and not just used, in interstate commerce. This is so even if the actual use is only in intrastate commerce.[10] Second, the device must actually involve a game of chance. Thus a court overruled the Commission and declared a particular "pull-tab" scheme not to be a lottery because nothing had to be paid for the privilege of pulling the tab and the value received would be equal to the amount of money contributed.[11] In another case, however, a court affirmed a Commission order where the consumer paid 5 cents for a presumed 5 cents' worth of candy but enjoyed the possibility of receiving several times that amount. In the view of the court, "to remove all possibility of loss would make more effective the incentive to play, by removing the most forceful natural reason to refrain."[12]

It may be difficult to determine, especially in the candy industry, whether the manufacturer who packages or assembles the merchandise is contributing to the formation of a lottery device which is to be utilized later by a distributor. For example, if a box of candies of uniform size and shape contains one piece of candy with a different-colored center, this fact could be made the basis for a lottery. Should the Commission prohibit candy arrangements by manufacturers which "may be used" or "are designed to be used" or are "likely to be used" for a lottery? Regardless of differences on this score, especially as it concerns a court's thinking about what language is permissible in cease and desist orders, the Commission has stated that it is not the intention of the Commission or the courts to prevent manufacturers from selling candies just because a distributor might later sell them by means of a lottery device.[13] It is obvious that the Commission has to examine the intent.

The lottery devices prohibited by the Federal Trade Com-

[9] *Federal Trade Commission v. Bunte Bros., Inc.,* 312 U.S. 349 (1941).

[10] *Zitserman v. Federal Trade Commission,* 200 F.2d 519 (1952).

[11] *J. C. Martin Corp. v. Federal Trade Commission,* 242 F.2d 530 (1957).

[12] *Federal Trade Commission v. F. A. Martoccio Co.,* 87 F.2d 561, 564 (1937).

[13] *Samuel Worth d/b/a Worthmore Sales Company,* 46 F.T.C. 606 (1950).

mission have been diverse. The colored-center candy method, already mentioned, is one. A similar method is to differentiate the color of the piece of the candy where wrappings cover the candy color. Having a series of cards within candy wrappers provides the operator of the lottery with the opportunity of offering a prize for a collection of a minimum of twenty-five different cards. The price of the good itself may be made known only after the good has been unwrapped. Prizes may be present inside the wrapper. Punch boards, push or pull cards, or pull tabs can determine how much or what species of merchandise the chance-taker will obtain for a given amount of money or how much money he will have to pay for a given amount of goods. "Club" schemes in which members contribute a certain amount each involve the drawing of lots to see which members get what merchandise. The practice of giving coupons redeemable in various prizes or premiums of unequal value has been prohibited where the distribution was determined by chance.

Whereas the number of lottery schemes may be relatively small, the number of variations on these themes is legion. This general principle indubitably applies to the unfair selling practices which we have discussed in this chapter. And in this principle we have the justification, indeed the necessity, for the general language of Section 5 of the Federal Trade Commission Act.

## SUGGESTIONS FOR FURTHER READING

The work of the Federal Trade Commission in combatting deceptive selling and advertising can be followed in the Commission's *Advertising Alert* (monthly) and *News Summary* (approximately weekly). *Consumer Reports,* in addition to reporting on product testing, often carries articles on deceptive selling, e.g., "The Great Ham Robbery," March, 1961. Short articles on deceptive selling can be found in the *Reader's Digest:* "Five Swindles to Watch Out For," August, 1958; "The Cruelest Swindle in Medical 'Cures,'" June, 1960; "Unproved Cancer 'Cures' Can Cost Lives," September, 1961; and "Watch Out for Phony Household Repairmen," January, 1962. Also, in *The Saturday Evening Post:* "Don't Fall for the Mail Frauds," Mar. 29, 1958; and "Beware the Advance Fee Racket," Dec. 20, 1958. A summary of fraudulent selling to consumers is to be found in Leland J. Gordon, *Economics for Consumers,* 4th ed., American Book Company, New York, 1961, chap. 11. T. Swann Harding surveys fraudulent selling, including historical retrospect, in *The Popular Practice of Fraud,* Longmans, Green & Co., Inc., New York, 1935.

Extensive testimony and some data on payola in radio and television is available in the *Hearings of the Subcommittee on Payola and Other Deceptive Practices in the Broadcasting Field of the House Committee on Interstate and Foreign Commerce, Responsibilities of Broadcasting Licensees and Station Personnel,* 86th Cong., 2d Sess., 1960, parts I and II. *Consumer Protection Activities, Regulation of Weights and Measures by State and Local Governments, Hearings of the Subcommittee of the House Committee on Government Operations,* 87th Cong., 2d Sess., 1962, part I, is a source of information on deceptive weight and measure selling.

# 7

# *TRADE REGULATION REEXAMINED*

Trade regulation is a necessary concomitant of the free enterprise economy, to assure the maintenance of free and effective competition. The Sherman Antitrust Act of 1890, prohibiting restraints of trade and monopolizing, lies at the heart of the legal framework of the free enterprise competitive system. The basic principle underlying this act is that business firms should be able to operate in the marketplace free of restraints by other firms. The competition must be free to all, not just to those who can exert market power. One firm should be able to prevail over another only on the basis of economic efficiency. Such competition encourages the use of the best possible means of production and distribution of goods and services. The Clayton Act of 1914 supplemented the Sherman Act by declaring price discrimination, tying contracts, and the acquisition of the capital stock of another corporation to be unlawful where they might substantially lessen competition or tend to create a monopoly—the design of this act was to catch monopoly in its incipiency, before any damage could be done.

The Federal Trade Commission Act of 1914 gave further support to the basic concept underlying the Sherman Act. It established the Federal Trade Commission, which was to be a body of specialists which might deal with the economic and technical matters pertaining to restraints on competition. This act also condemned "unfair methods of competition," which came to be interpreted over time as including not only restraints on the competition which might tend toward monopoly but also those deceptive acts or practices which, even though they might not lead to monopoly, were injurious either to business firms or to the consumer. Misrepresentation and deception, especially in selling, can be injurious to the competition itself as well as to the consumer who is being deceived, for profits derived therefrom are not profits resulting from economic efficiency. The process of competition becomes distorted. And, in order to survive, competitors may be forced to follow the lead of others who have adopted such means of competition.

From time to time additional legislation has been passed to provide further controls over both restraints of trade and deceptive practices. The additions to and changes in trade regulation law have come slowly, as the need for new legislation has become strongly felt. The body of trade regulation law which has evolved is largely negative, but it has some positive aspects, especially with respect to labeling requirements.

Trade regulation in the United States is neither a perfect nor an entirely consistent system of social control. Some of its weakness is inherent because it is largely a negative system of regulation in a democracy, spelled out in large part in general terms. Other weaknesses, however, are in the statutes themselves, as legal efforts to maintain competition have been undermined by provisions of law which do not contribute to a basic, well-integrated, legal framework. Some statutory provisions have the effect of restricting the full freedom of some business firms to compete. Fair trade, written at law as being an exemption from our basic antitrust laws, is the result of certain business interests persuading legislators that competition is being made freer and fairer to all competitors by enabling certain producers or distributors to control resale prices. The rationale of sales-below-cost laws is somewhat similar. The law of price discrimination, legitimately aimed at achieving competition which is free to the small competitor as well as to the large, has overachieved its purpose, at the cost of other competitors' legitimate freedom to compete. At the heart of the cause of this lack of integration or apparent inconsistency of the legal framework is an inability of all to agree on the precise nature of the competition to be desired and supported by public policy in markets which are not all uniform in structure.

## STATUTORY UNCERTAINTY

The nature of the basic antitrust statutes is to proclaim to the business community what its members cannot do. These statutes are worded in general terms. A certain degree of uncertainty about what is legal and what is illegal is inherent. The Sherman Antitrust Act of 1890, as interpreted by the courts, makes unlawful only unreasonable restraints of trade. But what is unreasonable is often a matter for further determination. Likewise, the Sherman Act declares monopolizing and attempts to monopolize to be illegal, but nowhere does the statute itself define these terms. Section 5 of the Federal Trade Commission Act uses the terms "unfair methods of competition" and "unfair or deceptive acts or practices." The Clayton Act condemns price discrimination, tying contracts, and the acquisition of stock or assets "where the effect may be substantially to lessen competition or tend to create a monopoly." The inclusion of the word "may" has led to a doctrine of reasonable probability. In litigation, therefore, these general words of the statutes require the production of much evidence and arouse considerable debate with respect to the relevancy of the evidence to the particular law. Business complains of this uncertainty and may argue, perhaps correctly, that it did not, or could not, know that it was violating the law.

This type of uncertainty of the law could be removed by making the law more specific. And this has been done in certain categories through court decisions which have established legal precedent making certain business practices illegal per se. Among otherwise independent firms collusive business behavior, such as agreements to fix prices, to restrict output, or to divide markets, is thus illegal per se. For such arrangements are made of the very cloth of monopoly. But to make all antitrust law specific is to risk introducing rigidities which may carry with them economic costs. To set limitations on the size of the firm and not permit it to merge, or grow, beyond that size, may prevent the achievement of economies of scale. To make exclusive dealing illegal in and of itself is to deny the benefits which may derive from such dealing under certain circumstances. And to make price discrimination illegal per se would deny such economies of scale as are inherent, for example, in quantity buying.

Some areas of trade regulation should be, and are, specific. Labeling requirements, either by statute or by rules promulgated by enforcement agencies, for foods, drugs, devices, cosmetics, certain wearing apparel, and hazardous substances can be positive and specific without restricting competition. It has been found from experience that where there are no positive labeling requirements the consumer and honest competitor are injured in a sufficient number of instances to make it necessary to protect them through such mandatory requirements.

## UNCERTAINTY OF JUDICIAL OPINION

The general wording of a statute provides considerable opportunity for differences of opinion in applying the law. Disagreement on the proper application of trade regulation law may exist at several possible levels of the judicial process. There have been split decisions among members of the quasi-judicial Federal Trade Commission. The Commission has overruled its hearing examiners. Courts of appeal have overruled the Federal Trade Commission. District courts have failed to support Department of Justice complaints. The Supreme Court has overruled lower courts. And certainly far from all the Supreme Court decisions have been unanimous. The opportunity to appeal a decision, for which the "due process" of law provides, can extend the uncertainty of the legality of a particular transaction or market practice over time. The alternative to this uncertainty, however, is the more arbitrary method of direct regulation.

Different interpretations undoubtedly are based partly upon the inherent predilections of the one who is standing in judgment. Thus the distinction between preserving a competitor, on the one hand, and preserving competition, on the other hand, may become lost in such predispositions. The whole purpose of the law may be seen in a particular light. Or, even further, a particular industrial structure may be viewed differently by different men. In the Standard Oil of California decision, which declared that exclusive dealing at the service-station level was illegal, there were two separate dissents. Justice Jackson, with Justice

Burton concurring, argued that, as far as he could see it without further evidence, the retail service stations were only a conduit between the oil fields and the automobile and that the exclusive dealing contracts were an almost necessary means of maintaining what was keen competition for the consumer business.[1] Justice Douglas argued against finding the exclusive dealing contracts illegal because, if they were to be outlawed, the major oil companies would take over the operation of the stations themselves, thus displacing the independent service-station operator. This would be "a tragic loss to the nation. The small independent businessman will be supplanted by clerks."[2]

## STATUTORY OBJECTIVE—FAIR TRADE

The fair trade laws of the states, supported by the Federal enabling legislation, are more in conflict than they are in agreement with the objective of maintaining competition equally free to all. Indeed, the Federal laws supporting the state resale price maintenance laws are explicitly presented, as amendments to the Sherman and Federal Trade Commission acts, as exempitons from the antitrust laws. Such exemptions represent a concession to private interests as represented first, by the desire of retailers to avoid price competition and second, by the protection of the property values of brands and trademarks of producers or distributors. The authority granted to the sellers of such branded goods extends beyond control of "loss-leader" selling; *all* price competition in the fair-traded goods is subjected to the control of the brand-name owner. To this degree, price reductions of these goods in favor of the consumer are thus restricted. Sales-below-cost laws also restrict competition, but are less objectionable than fair trade laws, for they establish minimum prices which are usually below what fair-trade minimum prices would be.

The Federal Trade Commission has opposed fair trade for two essential reasons.[3] First, it provides for the determination of

---

[1] *Standard Oil Company of California et al. v. United States*, 337 U.S. 293, 323 (1949).

[2] *Ibid.*, pp. 320–321.

[3] Statement of Paul Rand Dixon, Chairman, Federal Trade Commission, before the Senate Committee on Commerce, Oct. 9, 1963 (mimeographed).

resale prices by noncompetitive forces, i.e., a manufacturer or distributor, not the retailer who is selling the good to the public, sets the price. Second, fair trade does not promote maximum efficiency and lowest prices to the consumer. More precisely, the arguments of the Commission against fair trade are several. Tacit agreements among manufacturers are facilitated when prices are openly published and maintained over a considerable period of time. Low-cost distributors are prevented from passing on their savings to consumers. Higher rather than lower prices mean a lower volume of sales. Retailers' competition with lower-price, private-brand chains is restricted; the small businessman is hindered rather than helped in the competition. Fair-trade pricing may even induce increased use of private labels. And controlled retail prices may induce the competitors to indulge in costly nonprice methods of competition.

A growing number of state fair trade laws has been subjected in the late 1950s and the early 1960s to serious question and even rejection on constitutional grounds by state supreme courts. And speaking in opposition to bills which would create Federal fair trade have been the Federal Trade Commission, the Departments of Justice, Commerce, and Agriculture, and the Consumer Advisory Council. Political realities, however, are not reassuring that such new Federal legislation will not become a fact, as vested interests, often in the name of the preservation of small business, seek protection from full-fledged competition.

## STATUTORY OBJECTIVE—THE ROBINSON-PATMAN ACT

The basic objective of the antitrust laws is to prevent injury to competition. To distinguish between an injury to competition and an injury to a competitor is not easy, however. An injury to a competitor may represent an injury to competition. On the other hand, a competitor may be injured because he cannot survive competition. A firm can be forced out of business (or suffer reduced profits) because of downright inefficiency, because it is too small to achieve economies of scale, because it is not keeping up with technological change or marketing innovations, or because it is the victim of the market power inherent in the size of a larger firm. If competition is to be maintained by law, then the law should protect firms only from the last-mentioned factor.

To protect a firm beyond that by law introduces a new element into public policy, namely, the protection of business from competition.

The Clayton Act of 1914 stated that price discrimination was illegal where the effect may be to lessen competition substantially. Congress, however, became dissatisfied with the Clayton Act provision with respect to price discrimination. Whereas that provision found fairly ready application to predatory sellers' discrimination, it did not seem to reach so readily the power, and resulting discriminations, of the large buyer. In an effort to control the buying power of the larger firms, Congress passed the Robinson-Patman Act amendment to the Clayton Act. The Robinson-Patman Act attempted to meet the issue by spelling out the legality of discriminations in detail. The result has been a statute which, in its effort to control discriminations which were injurious to competition, has prevented discriminations whether they were lessening competition or not and which in some cases has reduced competition rather than increased it.

Provisions of the Robinson-Patman Act furnish evidence of a policy desire to protect small business firms against discrimination even at the possible cost of preserving inefficiency. First, the quantity limit proviso of Section 2(*a*) of the act gives the Federal Trade Commission the authority to establish quantity limits which would prohibit those price discounts which only a few firms, because of their size, would be able to take advantage of. Prohibition of such discounts, termed "unjustly discriminatory or promotive of monopoly," would deny possible economies of scale. The Sherman Act, in contrast, denies such economies only where the power inherent in such size is being abused.

Second, the brokerage clause of the Robinson-Patman Act, Section 2(*c*), prohibits absolutely the granting of brokerage or any allowance in lieu thereof to any party except an independent broker. This requirement means that no buyer can perform his own brokerage service and be remunerated for it. A buyer must pay the same price as all other buyers even though the services of a broker have not been involved. The only way that this restriction of the law can be avoided by a buyer is to deal with a seller who does not use the services of a broker at all. The brokerage clause thus introduces rigidity into the channels of distribution. The independent broker is in a preferred market position. And, paradoxically, under this provision cooperative buying groups of small businessmen have been denied remuneration for any services they may have performed. The removal of this clause from the act would represent an improvement in efforts to maintain competition by permitting greater flexibility of market action to buyers and sellers.

Third, Sections 2(*d*) and 2(*e*) require the giving of promotional allowances and the furnishing of services to all buyers on proportionally equal terms. This requirement seeks fair treatment for the small buyer. But the statute makes no reference to the cost to the seller in providing these allowances and services on a proportionally equal basis; nor does it require that a showing be made of injury to competition.

## STATUTORY CONSTRUCTION—THE ROBINSON-PATMAN ACT

The general and fairly simple wording of Sections 1 and 2 of the Sherman Act and Section 5 of the Federal Trade Commission Act can provide the framework for legal jousting, judicial disagreement, and resulting uncertainty. This, however, as we have pointed out, is a necessary characteristic of our antitrust laws. What is not justifiable, on the other hand, is a statute which is poorly worded and which contains subsections which do not clearly tie together to provide a cohesive statute. This has been a chief misfortune of the Robinson-Patman Act on price discrimination. It is made up of several subsections, the relationships between which have not been at all clear, and contains several qualifying clauses or provisos as well. It is, in short, "one of the most tortuous legislative pronouncements ever to go on the statute books."[4]

Disagreement in litigation can arise, therefore, not just over the application of the evidence to the law in a particular case, but rather over what the law itself means. It took fifteen years before the Supreme Court decided that the good faith proviso of Section 2(*b*) was a substantive defense to a charge of violating

[4] Joel B. Dirlam and Alfred E. Kahn, *Fair Competition: The Law and Economics of Antitrust Policy,* Cornell University Press, Ithaca, N.Y., 1954, p. 119.

Section 2(*a*) of the act; the Federal Trade Commission had proceeded on the assumption that it was merely a procedural defense in rebutting a prima facie case and that if there were an injury to the competition, the good faith defense was not enough to excuse the respondent. Even in 1963 there was disagreement among lower courts and the Federal Trade Commission about whether good faith can be used as an aggressive as well as a defensive tactic. The cost defense of Section 2(*a*) is apparently not available as a defense for reduced brokerage charges under Section 2(*c*), although there is now some doubt on this matter. It took court decisions to indicate that the good faith defense of Section 2(*b*) is available to justify unproportional granting of allowances of Section 2(*d*) and furnishing of services of Section 2(*e*). Does Section (2*f*) on buyer's liability apply to Sections 2(*d*) and 2(*e*) concerning the furnishing of promotional allowances and services? If it does, the statute does not say so. The omission of reference to "in commerce" in Section 2(*e*) has been ruled by a lower court to be a mere inadvertence. It took a court to rule that section 2(*e*) prohibits the furnishing of services to all competing purchasers on proportionally equal terms, not just to "all" purchasers, as the statute states. And, too, the act does not spell out proportional to what in Sections 2(*d*) and 2(*e*).

The solution for remedying the statutory structural defects is not to write more sections into the act. The faults undoubtedly came into being because Congress was trying to write too much detail into the law, trying to cover as many possible contingencies as possible and to make the law as "certain" as possible. Yet bills before Congress would extend this mistaken approach. For example, a bill has been filed to make functional discounts based on the character of the selling, not of the buying, of the purchaser mandatory unless the seller can affirmatively demonstrate that failure to do so will not substantially lessen competition. Another bill would prohibit vertically integrated companies from engaging in discriminatory practices against independent producers and distributors. Such bills would add to the confusion and probably introduce further rigidities into the economy. There is no doubt that the antitrust laws should include an effective statute against price discriminations, including those induced by the large buyer. But a less-detailed, more coherent, and better-integrated statute would be preferable to a law which, in its detail and extensiveness, only creates rigidities or uncertainties. This kind of uncertainty is avoidable. A statute like the Robinson-Patman Act, however, tends to become, in terms of political realities, an established institution to which additions are more easily made than deletions are.

## ADMINISTRATION OF TRADE REGULATION

Good administration by the enforcement agencies is a key to good trade regulation. Most offenses under trade regulation law come under the general headings of unreasonable restraint of trade, substantial lessening of competition, or unfair methods of competition. The enforcement agencies must apply a rule of reason. Some offenses, such as price-fixing, have become "hard core," or illegal per se. But many, if not most, are not; and questions such as what the relevant product market is, whether there has been good faith, or whether a discrimination can be cost-justified can be answered only after careful analysis. The more reasonable and consistent the enforcement agencies' interpretations in such matters, the more respected and more effective the trade regulation will be, and the greater the accord between the government enforcement agencies and business.

Where there is inherent uncertainty in the law, there are bound to be practices or conduct whose legality is in doubt. But with procedures which are especially designed to facilitate voluntary compliance available, and assuming that the enforcement agencies' position is reasonable, there is little reason for a constant parade of litigation. Certainly there is no excuse for continued violations through such practices as price-fixing and the use of lotteries, for in these areas public policy is clearly established. Where *new* market practices are involved, a much higher degree of uncertainty about the question of their legality will necessarily exist. And new practices or marketing methods are to be encouraged if they represent economies over existing methods. Perhaps, therefore, in the area of innovations litigation is inevitable, for both sides may feel strongly toward their position and legal precedent is lacking and must be established.

There are two sides in the matter of trade regulation enforcement. Business should actively seek to understand the laws the compliance with which is its responsibility. With thorough study, the uncertainty of the law may no longer seem to be quite so impenetrable. Legal precedent does exist to cover most basic situations, although the facts that the holdings of judicial decisions can sometimes be reversed and new angles to old situations can be found do not contribute toward greater certainty in the law. In addition to familiarizing themselves with the law, the larger firms should establish safeguards to ensure that all personnel are complying with their legal obligations. For them, a strong internal audit concerning trade regulation compliance is a must. An active effort by business to comply with the rules of law which govern the free enterprise system in which it professes to believe considerably eases the burden of enforcement.

## SUGGESTIONS FOR FURTHER READING

Suggestions on antitrust policy can be found in C. E. Griffin, "Needed: A Realistic Antitrust Policy," *Harvard Business Review*, November–December, 1956; J. G. Van Cise, "How to Live with Antitrust," *Harvard Business Review*, November–December, 1962; J. B. Dirlam and A. E. Kahn, *Fair Competition: The Law and Economics of Antitrust Policy*, Cornell University Press, Ithaca, N.Y., 1954; *Report of the Attorney General's National Committee to Study the Antitrust Laws*, Washington, 1955; and Carl Kaysen and D. F. Turner, *Antitrust Policy: An Economic and Legal Analysis*, Harvard University Press, Cambridge, Mass., 1959. For a description of the process by which conflicting ideas of Supreme Court justices are resolved into a decision, see Justice William J. Brennan, Jr., "Inside View of the High Court," *New York Times Magazine*, Oct. 6, 1963.

For highly adverse criticism of the antitrust laws or their administration, read critically Petro Sylvester, "The Growing Threat of Antitrust," *Fortune*, November, 1962; R. H. Bork and W. S. Bowman, Jr., "The Crisis in Antitrust," *Fortune*, December, 1963; and Lowell Mason (former Federal Trade Commissioner), *The Language of Dissent*, The World Publishing Co., Cleveland, 1959.

Jesse Markham shows how antitrust is impinging more and more upon day-to-day decision making in "Antitrust Trends and New Constraints," *Harvard Business Review*, May–June, 1963. Robert W. Austin objects to fair trade, minimum markup laws, and the cost aspects of the Robinson-Patman Act in "Let's Get Cost Pricing Out of Our Laws," *Harvard Business Review*, May–June, 1954. Walter Adams attempts to reconcile antitrust and fair trade in "Resale Price Maintenance: Fact and Fancy," *Yale Law Journal*, June, 1955. J. F. Barron points out disadvantages of adding to the Robinson-Patman Act in "Mandatory Functional Discounts: An Appraisal," *Journal of Business*, July, 1962.

Three case books available are S. Chesterfield Oppenheim, *Federal Antitrust Laws, Cases and Comments,* 2d ed., West Publishing Company, St. Paul, Minn., 1959; Louis B. Schwartz, *Free Enterprise and Economic Organization,* 2d ed., Foundation Press, New York, 1959; and Milton Handler, *Cases and Other Materials on Trade Regulation,* 3d ed., Foundation Press, New York, 1960.

Current developments can be followed in the "Legal Developments in Marketing" section of the *Journal of Marketing;* Commerce Clearing House, *Trade Regulation Reporter* (current year, looseleaf); articles in the *Antitrust Bulletin;* and Annual Reports of the Federal Trade Commission.

# *APPENDIX A*

## REFERENCES TO FEDERAL
## STATUTES AND DECISIONS

**ABBREVIATIONS**

| | |
|---|---|
| Fed. | *Federal Reporter.* Includes cases argued and determined in circuit courts of appeals and district courts through November, 1924 |
| F.2d | *Federal Reporter, Second Series.* Includes cases argued and determined in courts of appeals |
| F. Supp. | *Federal Supplement.* Includes cases argued and determined in district courts |
| F.T.C. | *Federal Trade Commission.* Orders and decisions of the Commission |
| Sup. Ct. | *Supreme Court Reporter.* Cases argued and determined in the United States Supreme Court, published by West Publishing Company, St. Paul, Minn. |
| Stat. | *Statutes at Large.* Federal statutes as originally passed |
| Trade Reg. Rep. | *Trade Regulation Reporter.* Commerce Clearing House |
| U.S. | *United States Reports.* Cases argued and determined in the United States Supreme Court, published by the Government Printing Office |
| U.S.C. | *United States Code.* Contains the general and permanent laws of the United States in force |

## REFERENCES

With the exception of the *United States Code,* the number preceding the abbreviation indicates the volume number, and the number following the abbreviation indicates the page number. With respect to the *United States Code,* the number preceding the abbreviation indicates the title number, and the number(s) following the abbreviation indicates the section number(s).

In the following references to Federal legislation mentioned in the text only the original statute is cited; amendments, where they are relevant, may be obtained from the U.S.C. reference.

Agricultural Marketing Agreement Act, 50 Stat. 246 (1937), as amended, 7 U.S.C. 671–672.

Anti-racketeering Act, 62 Stat. 793 (1948), 18 U.S.C. 1951.

Automobile Dealer Franchise Act (Automobile Dealers' Day in Court Act), 70 Stat. 1125 (1956), 15 U.S.C. 1221–1225.

Automobile Information Disclosure Act, 72 Stat. 325 (1958), 15 U.S.C. 1231–1233.

Capper-Volstead Act (Cooperative Marketing Associations Act), 42 Stat. 388 (1922), 7 U.S.C. 291–292.

Celler-Kefauver Act (Antimerger Act, amending Section 7 of Clayton Act), 64 Stat. 1125 (1950), 15 U.S.C. 18.

Clayton Act, 38 Stat. 730 (1914), as amended, 15 U.S.C. 12–27.

Co-operative Marketing Act, 44 Stat. 802 (1926), 7 U.S.C. 451–455.

Defense Production Act, 64 Stat. 798 (1950), 50 U.S.C. App. 2158, 2166.

Federal Alcohol Administration Act, 49 Stat. 981 (1935), as amended, 27 U.S.C. 205.

Federal Aviation Act, 72 Stat. 769 (1958), 49 U.S.C. 1381.

Federal Food, Drug, and Cosmetic Act, 52 Stat. 1040 (1938), as amended, 21 U.S.C. 301–392.

Federal Hazardous Substances Labeling Act, 74 Stat. 372 (1960), 15 U.S.C. 1261–1273.

Federal Trade Commission Act, 38 Stat. 717 (1914), as amended, 15 U.S.C. 41–58.

Fishermen's Collective Marketing Act, 48 Stat. 1213 (1934), 15 U.S.C. 521–522.

Flammable Fabrics Act, 67 Stat. 111 (1953), as amended, 15 U.S.C. 1191–1200.

Food and Drug Act, 34 Stat. 768 (1906), as amended; see Federal Food, Drug, and Cosmetic Act.

Fur Products Labeling Act, 65 Stat. 175 (1951), 15 U.S.C. 69–69j.

Lanham Trademark Act (cancellation provision), 60 Stat. 433 (1946), as amended, 15 U.S.C. 1064, 1115.

McCarran-Ferguson Act (Insurance Regulation Act), 59 Stat. 33 (1945), 15 U.S.C. 1011–1015.

McGuire-Keogh Act (amending the Federal Trade Commission Act), 66 Stat. 631 (1952), 15 U.S.C. 45.

Merchant Marine Act, 41 Stat. 988 (1920), 46 U.S.C. 885.

Miller-Tydings Act (amending Sherman Antitrust Act), 50 Stat. 693 (1937), 15 U.S.C. 1.

Packers and Stockyards Act, 42 Stat. 159 (1921), as amended, 7 U.S.C. 181–229.

Perishable Agricultural Commodities Act, 46 Stat. 531 (1930), as amended, 7 U.S.C. 499*a*, 499*b*.

Revenue Act (antidumping provisions), 39 Stat. 798 (1916), 15 U.S.C. 71–74.

Robinson-Patman Act (Price Discrimination Chain Store Act, amending Clayton Act), 49 Stat. 1526 (1936), 15 U.S.C. 13–13*b*, 21*a*.

Securities Act, 48 Stat. 74 (1933), as amended, 15 U.S.C. 77*a*–77*aa*.

Sherman Antitrust Act, 26 Stat. 209 (1890), as amended, 15 U.S.C. 1–7.

Tariff Act (marking of imported articles and containers), 46 Stat. 687 (1930), as amended, 19 U.S.C. 1304.

Tariff Act (unfair practices in import trade), 46 Stat. 703 (1930), as amended, 19 U.S.C. 1337.

Textile Fiber Products Identification Act, 72 Stat. 1717 (1958), 15 U.S.C. 70–70*k*.

Webb-Pomerene Act (Export Trade Act), 40 Stat. 516 (1918), 15 U.S.C. 61–65.

Wheeler-Lea Act (amending Federal Trade Commission Act), 52 Stat. 111 (1938), 15 U.S.C. 45, 52–58.

Wilson Tariff Act, 28 Stat. 570 (1894), as amended, 15 U.S.C. 8–11.

Wool Products Labeling Act of 1939, 54 Stat. 1128 (1940), 15 U.S.C. 68–68*j*.

# APPENDIX B

## EXCERPTS FROM ANTITRUST STATUTES

**SHERMAN ACT**

SEC. 1. Every contract, combination in the form of trust or otherwise, or conspiracy, in restraint of trade or commerce among the several States, or with foreign nations, is hereby declared to be illegal. Every person who shall make any such contract or engage in any such combination or conspiracy, shall be deemed guilty of a misdemeanor, and, on conviction thereof, shall be punished by fine not exceeding fifty thousand dollars, or by imprisonment not exceeding one year, or by both said punishments, in the discretion of the court.

SEC. 2. Every person who shall monopolize, or attempt to monopolize, or combine or conspire with any other person or persons, to monopolize any part of the trade or commerce among the several States, or with foreign nations, shall be deemed guilty of a misdemeanor, and, on conviction thereof, shall be punished by fine not exceeding fifty thousand dollars, or by imprisonment not exceeding one year, or by both said punishments, in the discretion of the court. [NOTE: Maximum fines were raised from $5,000 to $50,000 by amendment in 1955.]

## FEDERAL TRADE COMMISSION ACT

SEC. 5. Unfair methods of competition in commerce, and unfair or deceptive acts or practices in commerce, are hereby declared unlawful.

## CLAYTON ACT

SEC. 3. That it shall be unlawful for any person engaged in commerce, in the course of such commerce, to lease or make a sale or contract for sale of goods, wares, merchandise, machinery, supplies or other commodities, whether patented or unpatented, for use, consumption or resale within the United States or any Territory thereof or the District of Columbia or any insular possession or other place under the jurisdiction of the United States, or fix a price charged therefor, or discount from, or rebate upon, such price, on the condition, agreement, or understanding that the lessee or purchaser thereof shall not use or deal in the goods, wares, merchandise, machinery, supplies or other commodity of a competitor or competitors of the lessor or seller, where the effect of such lease, sale, or contract for sale or such condition, agreement, or understanding may be to substantially lessen competition or tend to create a monopoly in any line of commerce.

SEC. 7. That no corporation engaged in commerce shall acquire, directly or indirectly, the whole or any part of the stock or other share capital and no corporation subject to the jurisdiction of the Federal Trade Commission shall acquire the whole or any part of the assets of another corporation engaged also in commerce, where in any line of commerce in any section of the country, the effect of such acquisition may be substantially to lessen competition, or to tend to create a monopoly. . . .

This section shall not apply to corporations purchasing such stock solely for investment and not using the same by voting or otherwise to bring about, or in attempting to bring about, the substantial lessening of competition. Nor shall anything contained in this section prevent a corporation engaged in commerce from causing the formation of subsidiary corporations for the actual carrying on of their immediate lawful business, or the natural and legitimate branches or extensions thereof, or from owning and holding all or a part of the stock of such subsidiary corporations, when the effect of such formation is not to substantially lessen competition.

## ROBINSON-PATMAN ACT, AMENDING SECTION 2 OF THE CLAYTON ACT

SEC. 2. (a) That it shall be unlawful for any person engaged in commerce, in the course of such commerce, either directly or indirectly, to discriminate in price between different purchasers of commodities of like grade and quality, where either or any of the purchases involved in such discrimination are in commerce, where such commodities are sold for use, consumption, or resale within the United States or any Territory thereof or the District of Columbia or any insular possession or other place under the jurisdiction of the United States, and where the effect of such discrimination may be substantially to lessen competition or tend to create a monopoly in any line of commerce, or to injure, destroy, or prevent competition with any person who either grants or knowingly receives the benefit of such discrimination, or with customers of either of them: *Provided,* That nothing herein contained shall prevent differentials which make only due allowance for differences in the cost of manufacture, sale, or delivery resulting from the differing methods or quantities in which such commodities are to such purchasers sold or delivered: *Provided, however,* That the Federal Trade Commission may, after due investigation and hearing to all interested parties, fix and establish quantity limits, and revise the same as it finds necessary, as to particular commodities or classes of commodities, where it finds that available purchasers in greater quantities are so few as to render differentials on account thereof unjustly discriminatory or promotive of monopoly in any line of commerce; and the foregoing shall then not be construed to permit differentials based on differences in quantities greater than those so fixed and established: *And provided further,* That nothing herein contained shall prevent persons engaged in selling goods, wares, or merchandise in commerce from selecting their own customers in bona fide transactions and not in restraint of trade: *And provided further,* That nothing herein contained shall prevent price changes from time to time where in response to changing conditions affecting the market for or the marketability of the goods concerned, such as but not limited to actual or imminent deterioration of perishable goods, obsolescence of seasonal goods, distress sales under court process, or sales in good faith in discontinuance of business in the goods concerned.

(*b*) Upon proof being made, at any hearing on a complaint under this section, that there has been discrimination in price or services or facilities furnished, the burden of rebutting the prima facie case thus made by showing justification shall be upon the person charged with a violation of this section, and unless justification shall be affirmatively shown, the Commission is authorized to issue an order terminating the discrimination: *Provided, however,* That nothing herein contained shall prevent a seller rebutting the prima facie case thus made by showing that his lower price or the furnishing of services or facilities to any purchaser or purchasers was made in good faith to meet an equally low price of a competitor, or the services or facilities furnished by a competitor.

(*c*) That it shall be unlawful for any person engaged in commerce, in the course of such commerce, to pay or grant, or to receive or accept, anything of value as a commission, brokerage, or other compensation, or any allowance or discount in lieu thereof, except for services rendered in connection with the sale or purchase of goods, wares, or merchandise, either to the other party to such transaction or to an agent, representative, or other intermediary therein where such intermediary is acting in fact for or in behalf, or is subject to the direct or indirect control, of any party to such transaction other than the person by whom such compensation is so granted or paid.

(*d*) That it shall be unlawful for any person engaged in commerce to pay or contract for the payment of anything of value to or for the benefit of a customer of such person in the course of such commerce as compensation or in consideration for any services or facilities furnished by or through such customer in connection with the processing, handling, sale, or offering for sale of any products or commodities manufactured, sold, or offered for sale by such person, unless such payment or consideration is available on proportionally equal terms to all other customers competing in the distribution of such products or commodities.

(e) That is shall be unlawful for any person to discriminate in favor of one purchaser against another purchaser or purchasers of a commodity bought for resale, with or without processing, by contracting to furnish or furnishing, or by contributing to the furnishing of, any services or facilities connected with the processing, handling, sale, or offering for sale of such commodity so purchased upon terms not accorded to all purchasers on proportionally equal terms.

(f) That it shall be unlawful for any person engaged in commerce, in the course of such commerce, knowingly to induce or receive a discrimination in price which is prohibited by this section.

# CASE INDEX

# SUBJECT INDEX